I0153224

Black is White

My Experiences as a Jesuit Priest

Michael Matthew Casey

Table of Contents

Copyright

Published by Bark Louder Publishing
info@barklouder.com

http://www.barklouder.com/publishing

ISBN: 978-0-9851580-3-3

1.   Catholic Church Abuse—Memoir. 2. Irish Catholic—Non-fiction. 3. Catholic Church—Non-fiction. 4. Catholic Church Abuse—Non-fiction. 5. Memoir—Catholic Church—Non-fiction.

Acknowledgments

Thank you to my sister, Margaret, for pushing this through.

Everything you know is wrong.

--Firesign Theater

INTRODUCTION

I am the most qualified guy around to describe the sacerdotal sodomy scandals in the Catholic Church and in the Jesuit religious order of recent decades.

I speak from experience, resentment, and clarity: raped at age thirteen by a pederast in a bunkhouse in the dark of night on a farm in North Dakota, a near victim of Father Michael Toulouse, S.J. at Gonzaga High School in 1950, humped by Father Gene Legault, S.J. in his room at a Jesuit seminary in 1958 while I was intoxicated. Denial of all this, and more denial carried me along through the fifteen years of Jesuit Training.

Toward the end of my career of shame and denial, a Cuban Jesuit, Oscar Mendez, pried me open one evening while we were smoking Canadian cigarettes and sipping some cheap altar wine which

I had lifted from the community cellar. I had been in the Jesuit Order for ten years.

It was evident to him that I was a suppressed and tortured male sexpot. By then I was nearly demented by shame, lies, and guilt.

A few years after Oscar made me honest, a merciful and proficient Catholic woman insisted that I get in bed with her. After that the shame and the lies seemed to abate.

Yeah, I had all these unwilling experiences. And so far I have not mentioned old fashioned adultery. I had a front row seat in the pre-Vatican II Church. You should listen to me.

I was a member of the Jesuit Order for seventeen years: August 1952 to April 1969, from age 18 to age 35. Then I left the Church in 1969, got married, had two children, was divorced, taught in public schools and paid child support, avoided all social causes, believed that the entire Jesuit humiliation and Church hypocrisy would just drop into its appointed pit of reactionary stagnation. I was rid of it. What need of me to bear witness to the Church's hysteria? I had a life: impoverished and embittered, but a life.

Then, out of curiosity, I tuned into the Priestly Pederasty News Channel. At first, it nauseated me. Then, it embarrassed me (did people think I was one of them!), then it was burning resentment against the Church and the Jesuits. Old and sour memories came back. God! how I resent those people.

It does seem, doesn't it, that a nasty sacerdotal sodomy case hits the headlines every month. Just now, in Portland, Oregon, the cops arrested a priest for molesting some youngster. The priest was booked and indicted.

Bravo Cops! This, you see, represents some progress over the practice of blaming the victim. This was a big change in law enforcement even from five to ten years ago. I'm thinking, maybe there is some hope for honesty in the Church. May we hope that the District Attorney ignored Church Law and followed Civil Law!

But two days later, the headlines say: Archdiocese of Portland hires the most expensive criminal lawyer in the State of Oregon to defend the priestly pederast. This is the same diocese that had to declare bankruptcy because it could not afford to pay off the victims of previous priestly pederasts. How is it possible for anyone to say that the Church is reforming itself? Fat lawyer fees for Father Pederast, chicken feed for the victims.

It was the chancellor of the Portland Archdiocese who made the startling announcement that he had hired the most expensive criminal lawyer in Oregon to defend the priest. Then he made an apology to the youngster's family, and also to the parish where the molestation took place.

But here's the catch. The Archbishop was not present at the public apology. The Archbishop, the Reverend Klaus von Chickenkisser, was back at his residence watching re-runs of "Gunsmoke" and "Bugs Bunny".

People ask me why I left the Jesuits. I tell them, "You got it wrong. The question is: why did I stay so long?" Long was seventeen years after I turned eighteen.

Why did I stay so long? The answer is simple: sheer ignorance. I mean wall-to-wall ignorance. I mean no-relief-in-sight ignorance. I mean I just did not know-any-better-ignorance. Maybe it was even voluntary ignorance. The kind of ignorance I'm talking about does not only mean that a healthy boy has not only vague ideas about what men and women do in the bedroom, or has fantasy notions about pregnancy and childbirth. It means that Mama and Papa never mention the subject. Nor do the neighbor kids. Nor does anyone.

This ignorance means that nothing real or serious can ever be discussed.

Before Vatican II, and indeed for many years after, the Church preachers stood in the pulpit on Sunday and proclaimed that young girls and boys are not to be educated together, for that would be an occasion of sin. The celibate preacher fears that a snakey guy might reach across the aisle while the teacher faces the blackboard and, terrible to say, might squeeze a titty. If caught, the horny rascal would be denounced and condemned to say the rosary every night for fifteen years.

O.K. Sexual ignorance might seem to be the same as run-of-the-mill sexual repression. As I use the terms, individuals suffer from sexual repression and dysfunction. Whereas, sexual ignorance means that the entire People of God are on your case. Indeed, on everyone's case.

To rid yourself of sexual repression, perhaps an individual might make a visit or two to a sex therapist. The hang-ups can be alleviated or managed. However, to rid yourself of sexual ignorance, you have to dump the entire Church and its presumed moral authority.

For example, a few months before I finally left the Church and the Jesuits altogether, a young man often came to me to confess his sins. Actually all he had to confess was masturbation. As I got nearer to leaving the Church myself, I finally dared to tell him not to confess his many masturbations anymore. "It's simply not a sin," I said. "It's a completely natural act. Think of it on the same level as blowing your nose. The pleasure you feel from masturbation is just the relief your body experiences from testicular and penile tension." I don't know if what I said was of any help to him. But it felt right for me to say this if only to confront my own hypocrisy about masturbation.

I had arrived at my own conclusions on the subject several years before. However, I told no one, and certainly not in the confessional, that masturbation was not a sin at all. I knew I was right but lacked confidence in my judgment. This lack of confidence I attribute to sexual ignorance. It involved years of hiding from reason, truth, and honesty. Also, there was lack of courage to tell the other priests lurking nearby to just shove it if they challenged me on the subject.

The sacerdotal sodomy scandal did not sneak up on the Church from a few sick sacerdotals. It came, and is still coming, from the

Church itself and its self-proclaimed mission that it alone can speak for God Almighty. God speaks from the mouth of the Great Pig. The Great Pig declares himself infallible in faith and morals. For example, the Church considers pederasty unnatural. But if a priestly pederast is reported to some authority or other, the Church will slip into Tammy Wynette posture, and "stand by" her priest, and forbid any traffic with the local District Attorney. The Church's law is "above" civil law. To hand the priest over to civil authorities would be tantamount to admitting that the Catholic Church, and its Supreme Pontiff, does not possess supreme and complete authority over all people and the entire earth.

Consider the question of abortion: many years after Betty Frieden's book, The Feminine Mystique, many liberated women still hem and haw about the "morality of abortion." So, who made it an issue? What organized force put this doubt into the minds of so many women? Was this a group of women, organized or disorganized? Or, perhaps it was a very well organized Klan of Kluless Kardinals? Could be.

Here's another example: it used to be that Gloria Steinem – a role model of liberation – often got her picture in the New York

Times. But now, hardly ever. But just count up the times you saw the picture of that fat and very wealthy Cardinal Tim Dolan preening before the Republican Convention, honoring that smuck of smucks, Mitt Romney. Catholics and Mormons united in the tax-exempt family values take-over of America. (Hey, they already have the Supreme Court, six to three.)

Picture the hooded hierarchs deciding what persons can be married, what can be taught in any school, public or private, about sex education, whether gays or lesbians can get married, or whether they can even love each other, whether anyone, ever, can use a condom.

Any topic or issue from the region south of the belly button to the upper thighs of a human being is the exclusive property of the Catholic Church. Our Holy Father has his hand on the groin of the entire world. Papal territories indeed!

But before he got his mitts on anyone's genitals, the Great Pig snuck into your noggin when you were baptized at the age of two weeks. "In the name of the Father, the Son, and the Holy Sexual Ignorance," intones the priest. The baptismal water flows over your innocent noggin, and from there onward to your first communion, the confession of sins, catechism classes, and – oh – lest I forget, always

14

respect for the priest, an unmarried man in a black suit with indeterminate carnal ignorance, and sometimes with whiskey on his breath.

Then the bishop comes to town in his limousine and driver (also in a black suit). His presence in the village means that it is time for the Sacrament of Confirmation. From this you will emerge as a soldier of Christ. The bishop confirms each kid individually. The Sacrament (a holy seal) is completed when he taps you on the cheek. He does this, and you notice the gold cuff links on his starched shirt. Well, you are impressed. This is clerical status and you promise Our Lord to change your socks every week! You are a soldier of Christ, defending the Kingdom of Rome.

But you have to pay for all of this. Here is a point of view you should consider: the Catholic Church has dozens, if not hundreds of religious congregations, for men and women. Also, there are the religious Orders, the Jesuits, the Franciscans, the Benedictines, the Dominicans. This entire swarm of chaste and inviolate men and women, like gnats in a swamp in Missouri or Siberia, have vowed never even to look at, let alone touch their genitals. Such unnatural vows produce entire oceans of guilt, never to be drained simply by leaving the Church. You have to give up the idea of Church reform and totally repudiate this whore of Babylon.

Maybe you do believe in Church reform, that once again the Spirit of Christ can return to Rome. Sure, and maybe Hitler will give up his gas ovens and sell his supply of Zyklon-B, and give the money to the poor. But there is more.

Besides teaching young people their ABCs, nuns and young men are taxed in real dollars when they enter their respective religious orders. The Church calls this a dowry. But it is an nonrefundable tax on their "vocations." When my sister Margaret joined the convent, my parents, who lived from month to month on very small paychecks, were assessed five hundred dollars, upfront. That was in 1956. Her religious order still has its mitts on that dough, plus all the compounded interest accrued in some tax-exempt bank account. Then she taught school in snotty Catholic schools for twenty years. The Order gets rich from her labor, and the labor of thousands of other nuns. Then she leaves the Order in the middle of the night, penniless. Will the Church ever give back her original dowry? Or any back pay? You think? All those nuns and all that tax-free dough is only one way the Catholic Church is still the wealthiest corporation in the world. I haven't even mentioned its millions of acres of tax-free real estate with massive multi-storied buildings for its colleges and law schools.

And how about that two thousand dollar cash scholarship I handed over to the Jesuits when I joined the Jesuits in 1952? It was from the Phillips Sixty-Six Petroleum Company in Bartlesville, Oklahoma. Only those graduating seniors were eligible whose parent worked at the company. I took a competitive exam and was one of twenty such seniors nationwide. I received four checks for five hundred dollars each for four years. The checks were made out to me personally. I signed each one over to the Father Rector. Once he actually thanked me, with his usual rictus-smile on his lips. Sixty-one years later, the Jesuits are still getting interest money from my original scholarship.

By the time I worked up the courage to split from the Jesuits, I had taught high school for four years, coached football and basketball, refereed hundreds of junior varsity games, erased blackboards forever, taught grade school at an Indian boarding school, and drove hundreds of miles in wheezing school busses filled with screaming Jesuit-hating mad-dogs.

In addition, I also taught philosophy for three years at Gonzaga and Seattle Universities. And hundreds of weekend sermons at various parishes, for which the Jesuits, not me, receive generous stipends.

When I left the Jesuits in the middle of the night, fearing the reproachful gaze of both students and Jesuits, my face was crimson red from the shame I felt from lifting a ten dollar bill from the collection basket. (But I needed bus fare to somewhere!) I wore a cheap black suit, a white tee shirt, scuffed black clerical shoes, carried a toothbrush with a change of underwear in a shopping bag, a well-thumbed paperback copy of Thomas Aquinas' Summa Theologicum. (This latter was in case I still suffered from shame-induced insomnia from betraying Our Lord by renouncing my vows. Phooey! Let Him continue bleeding to death for the greater glory of the sunken-faced pig-fuckers in Loyola's militia.)

You see, I was literally penniless. I was leaving peonage (take it or leave it) to penury (tough luck, meat-head).

You think there's money owing to me for back-pay, or perhaps some walking-out-the-door money?

Well, my fellow Americans who believe still in truth and justice, you just don't yet understand how the Jesuits got so wealthy. Zilch and Nada is what I got.

But who's bitter? Not me. A young man or woman marries the Church, takes a vow of poverty, and the Church gets rich and even richer.

CHAPTER 1: THE NEIGHBORHOOD OF BING CROSBY

The Casey family had moved from a homestead on the Fort Berthold Indian Reservation in North Dakota to Spokane, Washington. In actuality, my mother was the real driving force for this move. She wanted her kids to have a Catholic education. And, boy! did we get one.

After we settled in Spokane, the Caseys bought a house in St. Aloysius parish, God's personal ghetto. From our back porch, you could see Gonzaga University.

Figure 1Margaret, 1944

Figure 2Papa & Dominic

Figure 31942, North Dakota. Mama and four kids

St. Al's parish was started by Jesuit Indian missionaries about 1870. It was on the north bank of the Spokane River. The Indians were relocated to nearby reservations, and the Jesuits hung onto the best land and lots for their schools (for whites, not Indians). The school was named Gonzaga University.

Until 1954, Gonzaga High School was part of the University, same building, same teachers.

A word here about Aloysius Gonzaga himself. He was connected by several generations to Lucrezia Borgia. Small world, huh? Aloysius entered the Jesuits at age eighteen (as I myself did). He became a Jesuit, took some examinations in Latin, pronounced his vows at the age of twenty. Then he administered to the victims of the plague, and died at age twenty-two.

In no time at all, Aloysius Gonzaga became Saint Aloysius. The Church has thousands of saints but needs to restock its shelves every hundred years. The House of Gonzaga of Northern Italy had found its saint. It took a lot of money to pull it off. The House of Gonzaga wrote it off to the advertising budget. And the money is still rolling in. In fact, during basketball season, T.V. revenues from

Gonzaga University's yearly swagger into the Final Four funds many other sporting events, from golf (Bing Crosby, an alumnus is always pictured with a golf club in hand) and so on, even to student trips to sister colleges in South America. We thank thee, St. Al, our patron.

There are various portraits of St. Al, as he was called in the parish in Spokane. These show a pasty-faced, skinny and emaciated dum-dum. He was just the right role model to inspire healthy, vigorous, but sexually ignorant Michael Casey and others to join the Jesuit Order, and while eating well, take the three vows of Poverty, Chastity, and Obedience. Owing to the repression of the times, you daren't say, while looking at Al's picture, "My God, he's a fruit."

When the Jesuits were formed during the time of the Renaissance Italy, the Church was nothing but property, castles, and vast family dynasties. It was the original interlocking directorate. There were popes and cardinals everywhere. The popes often rode mules and horses, but more often mistresses. Many popes and cardinals had numerous children (which is just fine with me since I like youngsters) but the catch here is that if one of the kids was a boy, he was called a nephew, even the "papal nephew."

And also there was papal pluralism. If you did not like the pope in Rome, well, you could transfer your loyalty to another pope elsewhere, perhaps in Avignon, a fleshpot in southern France.

Aloysius Gonzaga had a great uncle named Francisco Borgia. This Borgia had inherited the original Borgia empire. The Borgia pope's less notorious son, Juan Borgia, became Duke of Gandia in Spain. Juan's son was Francisco Borgia. Francisco by about 1550 was second in power and wealth to the King of Spain himself.

Francisco had a large family and a sickly wife. When she died, he forsook his earthly dukedom, and all its wealth, and joined the Jesuit Order. Soon he is voted in as General of the Jesuit Order. More about this General stuff later, but you must remember that the Jesuits are a military order (no guns, but lots of poison). Thus, the title of General.

The Catholic Church does rule the world. I have given you the example of the Borgia dynasty running to Gonzaga University in Spokane. You're thinking that this is stretch. But have you considered that no taxes are paid for any Church-owned land? So, Gonzaga University pays no taxes. Over a time span of one hundred years, this accumulated to an enormous hunk of wealth. When I lived there, it was the second largest employer in Spokane. It owns acres and acres of prime real estate. It has warehouses and significant rents from them, and also from houses and businesses on land and lots which are leased from Gonzaga University.

Gonzaga University, under the guise of handing out college credits and diplomas, is actually an omnivorous corporation, dedicated to the accumulation of wealth, property, and avoidance of taxes. The Rothchilds are envious.

As to its world-wide influence, the Catholic Church rules by dynasties, families, and aspirants to the Knights of Malta, the Holy Knights of the Sepulchre of Jerusalem. In America, there is always the Knights of Columbus (who still own the land under the former Yankee Stadium).

Remember the T.V. program Firing Line, starring William B. Fuckley? Bill was a top guy in the Knights of Malta. His wife, Pat, was a Dame of Malta.

The Knights of Malta is known as the Catholic Billionaires Club and the Knights deserve the title. Another Knight, Bill Simon, was Nixon's Secretary of the Treasury. A few years ago his son ran for mayor of Los Angeles. John Foster Dulles' own son, Avery Dulles, became a Jesuit, and eventually a Cardinal in the Catholic Church. It's the dynasty angle.

On the local level, how does the Catholic Church rule the world? It's done by families with Jesuit sons and uncles doing surveillance on every corner of every block in all of Middle America. And certainly Spokane qualifies as Middle America.

St. Al's Parish in Spokane had produced more priests, novices, scholastics, and lay brothers per square mile than anywhere on the face of the earth. One house away from the Caseys on the corner of Indiana and Hamilton was the Church family with two sons, Dick and Pat, both in the Jesuits. A block away were the two Walsh brothers, Frank and Mickey, two blocks north was the home of Father Frank Duffy, S.J.; further west was the home of Father Michael Toulouse, S.J., and Father John Leary, S.J. (more about these pederasts later). Fr. Tom O'Brian, S.J., lived just three blocks away on Mission Avenue.

In time, the Casey family moved five blocks away, to Astor Street, and even closer to Gonzaga University. And wouldn't you know, across the street was the family of Father Bob Schiffner, S.J. He was the head of the French Department at Gonzaga University. And directly across the alley from our new home was the family of Bob Tanksley, S.J.

This is like Catholic and Jesuit carpet bombing. In ten square blocks I could name twenty other families with sons in the Order. It's like the apartment blocks in Moscow, with a KGB building superintendent on every floor. Who dares to question Stalin? Who dares to question the Pope or Bing Crosby? What happens is that you believe that your sexual ignorance is normal, and in time you will suffocate from lack of perspective. Your very frontal lobes seal up, you drool and mumble your prayers. You want to be a good little boy, hand your homework in on time, dedicate your life to the Sacred Heart of Jesus.

In St. Al's Parish, a "Jesuit" family stands guard on every block, ensuring the sexual ignorance of their sons. And every night the family prays for a Jesuit vocation for its oldest son. What chance did I have?

Every one of these families was obliged to purchase or to deliver door to door the Jesuit monthly publication, The Messenger of the Sacred Heart. This gem of saccharine devotion always featured on the cover the Great Bleeding Heart of Jesus Christ Himself. Inside it (the pamphlet, not the Great Heart) were lists of names of donors with

29

dollar amounts indicating who had contributed to the support of the Jesuit Order. And people did donate!

And what did these folk get for their donations? A request, next month, for more donations! Salvation for sale from the Great Bleeding Heart Himself.

Of course, the Sacred Heart of Jesus gets the last word. The Jesuits promote the Nine First Fridays. If a horny adolescent, on the First Friday of the month, confesses his sins, receives Holy Communion, and repeats this for the entire school year (nine months) he or she will be guaranteed absolution from all sins on his death bed. Such a deal! And his soul will go straight to heaven when he or she dies.

Was I the only imbecile that swallowed this con-job? There were millions of Catholic kids thus tormented. But think of the thousands of clergy who pushed this hoax. Imbeciles on one side and degenerate nihilists on the other side. All these neighborhood Jesuits were just like me and collectively this put a very tight clamp on my dick. Sexual ignorance was spread, like a plague, block by block, or clamp by clamp. Unless your parents told you otherwise, you couldn't escape from it. Every guy there, in high school or university, was taught that he had to at least consider joining the Jesuits, and were reminded that it was a mortal sin to refuse God's call.

These Jesuit sermons were delivered to us adolescents by reactionary Jesuit soldiers of Christ, the very same imbeciles who have forbidden sex education courses in any school, Catholic or public, and who have made a career out of calling the use of condoms a serious mortal sin. Eternal hell-fire for just one condom. Sure, Lord, I deserve it!

In time Michael Casey aspired to be one of these imbeciles. Was I sick? Absolutely not. In fact, I was normal. Keep in mind the cohesive force of neighborhood solidarity.

Once a friend of mine, Arnold Renner, invited me into his house. No one else was home. His sister and brother-in-law lived upstairs, and they also were not home. We went upstairs, and Arnold pulled open a dresser drawer. In it was a box of "rubbers", as condoms were then called. There were maybe a hundred rubbers in the box. I was mind-boggled by the immensity of this grave sin. A hundred fucks! Who could imagine so much carnal license?

We each lifted a few and left the house. We went to nearby Mission Park and enjoyed blowing them up like balloons. Arnold

Renner had an uncle in the Jesuit Order. Uncle Renner taught history at Gonzaga University. Did he know about the rubbers?

The next Sunday I went to confession before Mass and told the priest that I had played with certain nasty things. The priest thought I meant that I was playing with my dick. He gave me an entire rosary as penance. I thought that was very stiff – the penance, not my dick. I said the beads anyway. And in record time.

But the biggest enforcer of sexual ignorance of all was Bing Crosby. Bing had gone to Gonzaga University and was the best friend of a fellow student, Francis Corkery, S.J., the University's President. They were neighbors then and both played on the University's baseball team. Bing was second base and Corkery was shortstop.

Everyone in the parish knew that 508 East Sharp was the Crosby childhood home. It was exactly a block north of the University. Many of us walked by it as we went to school. It was a very large house. God Almighty, did we all feel privileged to be near the same space as der Bingle.

Bing had played a priest in "Going My Way" and "Bells of St. Mary's" and "I'm Dreaming of a White Christmas". The sanctity and sentimentality of these movies gushed down like silver dollars from heaven above. Every Catholic in the United States, until then a Protestant country, rejoiced in the notion that priests are really good guys and that it was O.K., even wonderful, to be a Catholic. And you could make your parents proud by joining the Jesuits.

So, how was der Bingle the biggest enforcer of sexual ignorance? He played a priest in movie after movie. der Bingle is a priest. Priests don't fuck. Hence you, Catholic youth, don't fuck! He was on the radio all day long. He was bigger than Sinatra. He sang wholesome songs like "If I knew you were coming, I'da baked a cake." He sang this with his horny adolescent son Gary.

The message from Bing was "I'm a really good guy. I went to Gonzaga and am donating millions to Gonzaga for a library. There will be no dirty books in it, with words like spermatozoa or erection. So, behave yourself and mind what the Jesuit fathers teach you. If you don't join the Jesuits yourself, at least don't marry a Protestant woman. Nah, don't even think about any women whatsoever. And if you complain, I'll turn your name into Cardinal Spellman or J. Edgar Hoover, the fairy. They both come to my Del Mar race track every summer. Fellow fairies."

In time I made friends with another kid named Joe Wallis. He was my age and nearly as ignorant as I was. All we talked about was "girls"; that is, what men and women did in the bedroom.

Joe assured me that he really knew what he was talking about.

Once Joe and I walked past the Mission Avenue grocery store on the corner behind his house. A pregnant woman walked from the store entrance to the corner, as Joe and I watched her. I still hadn't the foggiest idea as to what pregnancy meant or what it implied.

Joe set me straight. "Casey, you know the belly button?"

"Yeah?"

"Well, on a woman it opens real wide, wide enough for the kid to come out. Sometimes the doctor has to actually pull the baby out."

"The belly button? Really?"

"Would I shit you, Casey?"

"No, never."

It occurs to me now that perhaps Joe's sexual ignorance was worse than mine.

CHAPTER 2: FATHER COUGHLIN'S HARPOON

Gonzaga High School was part of Gonzaga University. During World War II, the U.S. Navy ran a V-12 program out of a set of old barracks, built pre-fab style. The Navy was gone and the barracks became Gonzaga High School. The place was dismal and creepy. It was perfect for fostering vocations to the Jesuits.

Classes were divided into four grades: 'A', 'B', 'C', and 'D'. These grades prevailed through all four years. The 'A' grade was the elite status. From it would emerge the future leaders of Christ's Kingdom.

I paid my 100 dollars tuition (saved from delivering newspapers and picking berries), took a test, and was assigned to the 'B' level. I was entirely comfortable there.

FR. JOHN COUGHLIN, S.J.
Latin, English, Algebra, Religion,
Class Teacher.

Figure 4 Class 1B, 1948

Each grade had a homeroom teacher. A homeroom teacher taught all of the subjects. These were Algebra, Latin, History, Religion, English, and study hall. The 1B room teacher was Father John Coughlin, S.J. You were in the room with him from 8:15 a.m. to 2:45 p.m. Forty-five minutes were allowed for lunch.

Father Coughlin was a fine teacher, but strange. He was tall, horse-face homely, a former college athlete in basketball and football.

Algebra was my best subject, then Latin, History so-so, Religion was just awful, English (Sir Walter Scott and Ivanhoe, blah; need I say more?).

In this stale reactionary setting, Father Coughlin's obsession was to give sex talks to fourteen year-olds on an individual basis. At the end of the day, as the class filed out of the room, he would snag a straggler, and detain him.

His right hand, with the shape and heft of a harpoon, shot out to the waist and belt of his prey. Inside the belt it went, the kid was immobilized. Then he sat at his desk while the kid stood like a calf roped by a Jesuit cowboy and then tied to a post.

By now his hand was inside the waistband but not far enough to reach the kid's nuts or dick. His thumb was still outside and over the belt, thus the appearances were saved. Coughlin had perfected the clamp and hold method of sex education.

By the standards of the time this was not pedophilia. But by God, it made you wonder, "What's next?"

Then came the questions, "Supposing you got your wife there on the bed. You gonna stick it into her?" Honest! I'm not making this up.

Then some moralistic b.s. would follow, like: "The seed is to make more Catholics. Do you know how to do that supposing you get the chance, you gonna do it?" Does my theme of sexual ignorance resonate with you?

We fourteen year-olds saw this, heard this, whispered among us. Our class motto was, "Supposing your wife..." This was sung to the tune of "Tantum Ergo, where'd your cock go?"

Everyone at Gonzaga High and probably Gonzaga University knew of this. Are we gonna complain? Go tell Father Toner, the school principal? You kidding? This was 1948, year one of the Great American Silence and Conformity. We took it as something that went with the territory. In fact I never heard of any parent complaining of this. Just who would blab this to Mom or Pop?

In time my turn came. Coughlin was waiting for me. I stood back from his desk and measured the length of his arm. Then I added a couple of feet. He read me as cautious about how far he could throw the harpoon. I looked at the door to the classroom. It was open. Should I bolt and run? But this would create a scene.

I managed to schmooze and groove through the "you gonna stick it in there?" interview. I was relieved that he did not lay a hand on me. So, I was given a pass, and went home to begin delivering the Spokane Daily Chronicle.

Even Jesuits allowed for some progress (o.k., just a little bit). At the end of the school year, some '1B' class kids would be moved up to the 'A' class. And some 'A' class kids would be moved down to the '1B' class.

Several times during the year, the sophomore '2A' class teacher Father Michael Toulouse, S.J. would come to the doorway of freshman 'B' class and chat with Father Coughlin. They looked us over during the afternoon study hall.

They exchanged ideas as to who of us hearties had the potential to take on the rigorous studies of Toulouse's elitist program in '2A'. Toulouse seemed especially interested in Jim Flynn, whose sister had been elected Miss Spokane the previous year. It seemed that Toulouse already knew Flynn. O.K., Jim was a very nice-looking young fourteen year-old.

In the fall of the next school year, 1949, four of us, Phil Thompson, Frank Vedalago, Jim Flynn, and Mike Casey were promoted to Toulouse's class in '2A'.

Classes began and our fate was sealed.

Brothers and Sisters in Christ, do you understand that Father Michael Toulouse, S.J. was an accomplished pederast?

CHAPTER 3: TOULOUSE, THE PEDERAST

Did anyone know? Of course not, certainly not me nor my mother, the monitor of my welfare. This is the fog of knowing and not knowing. Did Father Toner, the school principal and fine soldier of Christ, know? Did Father Francis Corkery, S.J., the University President and personal friend of Bing Crosby know? Of course not. No one knew. But surely some at the top of the Jesuit heap did know. How else could this infamy go forward (and still is going forward to this very day)?

FR. MICHAEL TOULOUSE, S.J.
Latin, Geometry, English, Religion, Class Teacher.

Figure 5 Michael Toulouse

FIRST ROW: Donald Barker, Jimmy Herlihy, Michael Steben, Jerry Schoenberg, Herbie McDonald, Thomas Vaugh. SECOND ROW: John Bowers, Michael Casey, Cy Rief, Jimmy Mertens, Herbert Sauvageau, Robert O'Brien, Bill McCarthy. THIRD ROW: Richard Leitch, John Walton, Max Wiltzius, Angus Kennedy, Jimmy Flynn, Phil Thompson, John Olson. FOURTH ROW: Peter Pauly, Frank Vedelago, Richard Winegard, Thomas Volk, John Gorman, Jimmy Brodersen, Armand DeFelice, Thomas Scott.

Figure 6Class 2A, 1949

Toulouse's program was to have his '2A' hotshots graduate in just three years instead of four. Thus he taught us two years of Latin in just one year, two years of Algebra in just one year, and two years of English in one year. As to History and Religion, well, the Jesuits didn't give a hoot about those subjects. All of these courses were demarcated into academic credits. All that remained for a '2A' hotshot was to complete his Junior year, and take a special class in English after school. Then the hotshot would graduate with Senior standing, and could move on to college (Gonzaga University, of course).

And through all of this, your sexual ignorance would be inviolate. Be patient now, I'll get to Toulouse the Pederast in a moment.

As to the two years in one year bullshit, that is what it was, just bullshit. The first Latin literature was Caesar's Gallic Wars. It was interesting and I could manage it, but in just one semester? Forget it. And Cicero, that nauseous windbag? It's not possible for an ordinary American boy (I was fifteen) to get those baffling complex paragraphs into any intelligible form. But it was even more baffling when you realized that Toulouse did not teach us a goddamn thing in Latin.

He told us to memorize Caesar's Gallic Wars at the rate of ten lines a day. In a month this really adds up. Caesar was not taught as literature but as scrimmage with tackling dummies. Caesar had an admirable prose style, but it was not examined.

Cicero's oration against Catiline (a Sicilian gangster) was simply impenetrable. Its opening line was "O! Tempora! O! Mores!" (Gee, the times, oh gee, the customs!) "Quo usque tandem abutere, Catiline, patientia nostra?" (How long, Catiline, will you abuse our patience?)

Never once was the class given a hint at the historical background and conditions of this literature. You need to remember that the Jesuits did not ever acknowledge that history itself is a force that gives some meaning to the study of the Classics. The Jesuits and the Church possessed the Truth of All Things regardless, thus history was irrelevant.

Toulouse's main job was to make us fifteen year-olds believe the elitist dogma that lay at the heart of Jesuit education. The dogma stated that we were the best, the elite.

Brothers and Sisters, don't look for this elitism now because Jesuits don't even teach their own system anymore. Before Vatican II, the system was Latin, Greek, English, Literature, History, Mathematics, and Speech or Classical Rhetoric. But now a family can run up a $100,000 bill to send a youngster to a Jesuit University or high school, and the kid will never have a Jesuit teacher. (Maybe the kid is lucky.)

O.K., perhaps the kid will have a Jesuit teacher in theology. But you know what theology is? It's jacking off in a bathtub. I'm not making this up. All theologians jack off in the bathtub.

Meanwhile, back to this elitist room '2A' stuff: Toulouse told everyone that he was just a fabulous teacher. And everyone believed him because he was so fabulous. And that's why we in '2A' were the best because as everyone knew, Toulouse was so fabulous, a great talker, very eloquent. Since we were in his class, it followed that we too were the best, the elite.

In reading this, if you aren't dizzy from it, then you have missed my point Then again, you might not be one of the elite. Perhaps you should re-memorize the orations of Cicero.

Now sixty-three years later, I am glad that I have a strong background in Latin and Greek. By his emphasis on these subjects, Toulouse set a high standard for us. I know I benefitted from it. But what was wrong about it was the bullshit of cramming two years of difficult studies into just one year. This ignores all understanding of adolescent and cognitive development. Besides, this "elite" business just plain goes against my egalitarian instincts.

And now my final blow: Toulouse's accelerated two years in one year program was not for our benefit. It was to glorify him, the fabulous Jesuit, who, it would soon be made clear, was also the premiere Jesuit pederast of the entire Northwest.

Even the Jesuits allowed for a parent-teacher meeting during the fall term of 1949. This was no doubt a concession to modern times. Of course my mother attended. She came home from the meeting and told me that Father Toulouse told her that her very own Michael was just a wonderful lad, so smart and so nice looking. She was aglow with maternal love and achievement. She told me this. And it increased my burden even beyond the ten lines of Caesar a day.

But I knew that some funny business lay ahead in '2A'. Am I gonna tell her that this is just Toulouse bullshit?

Well, even I believed it. I wanted to please Father Michael Toulouse, S.J., to be like his charismatic self. But am I a target? Did he say that to other mothers? After that I thought I might someday join the Jesuits. This is recruitment. What he had told Mama lowered my guard about him.

Why was my guard up in the first place? Toulouse roamed the classroom, translating from Caesar or teaching the various English figures of speech (at which he was a master). He would ask someone to stand and recite from memory the assigned ten lines a day of Caesar's Gallic Wars. Once he asked me to perform. I stood up and began the marathon. After about a hundred lines, he told me to sit down, so sweaty were my arm pits. Then he would roam around the classroom translating more Caesar or Cicero. He often sat with some kid in the kid's desk. This went on nearly every day. It made me very nervous. He never asked the kid to move over. He simply sat and bun-bumped the kid to the other side.

You're thinking, a Jesuit priest sitting with a fifteen year-old lad in his desk. What kind of behavior was this? I went to Gonzaga High for four years and I never saw any other Jesuit do this. Father Coughlin's harpoon hand on your belt was pushing it. And that was after school.

I noticed that there were some guys Toulouse never sat with for the bun-bumping exercise. On the other hand, there were about five or six guys he frequented. His favorites seemed to be Jim Flynn and Dick Leach.

I sat in the far corner of the room diagonal from the classroom door. You chose your desk on the first day of the school year and that was it for the next nine months.

This position was as far as I could get from Toulouse's front desk. The physicality of the room and Toulouse's omnivorous presence seemed to remind me of the bunkhouse in North Dakota when Bill Olson raped me in the dark of night. I'm not thinking of bolting from the room (the rest of the class would think I was nuts) but I don't feel like getting close to this guy. You just never know.

Across the aisle from me was Dick Leach. Dick was certainly the best looking kid in the class. Toulouse frequently sat with him. And Dick seemed, to me at least, at ease and suited to this sacerdotal supremacy. (Dick preceded me into the Jesuit Order.)

Then Toulouse began to sit with me as he translated the Gallic Wars. Remember, he didn't ask you to move over. He just sat and pushed with his hip and bun. When the period ended, he got up. Other guys nearby would grin at you or even smirk a bit. Did they know more about Toulouse than I did?

As I have mentioned, my only other experience of an adult male making physical contact on me was in a bunk house in North

Dakota in the Spring in 1948, when Bill Olson raped me in the night, while we were miles from nowhere. But this bun-bumping in '2A' is in broad daylight. Even so I felt an awful tension.

Toulouse was charismatic. Yet most of us were in fear of him. He would cut a guy in a flash. No one could predict when it was coming. This actually was a refinement of his predatory behavior. For example, Dick Wineguard sat in the back row. His pits were sweaty and he shivered a lot. Once Toulouse asked, "What's your first name, Wineguard?" The sweaty kid said, "Dick." Toulouse gratuitously said, "Well, you're a real dick, Wineguard." The laughter in the room was nervous. No guffaws. Anyone of us could be next.

I will say this for Toulouse: it was not possible to suck up to him. He had the strongest personality I ever met. I formed the idea that the only way I could match him was to join the Jesuit Order itself to save myself from utter inadequacy. All would be just swell if I were to join the elite, the Jesuits, God's Marines, the Pope's Green Berets. Oh! Shit! It was just awful. So, let's move on to the really smelly stuff.

In the middle of the year, Toulouse brings in Dave Morse from the freshman level. He announces that "I'm helping Davie with his Latin." The two of them sit together, hip to hip, in the very middle of

48

'2A'. This is during study hall from 1:30 p.m. to 2:15 p.m. The rest of us struggle with the Cartesian coordinates, the polynomials, the bloated Cicero and his attack on Catiline.

Catiline, an ancient despoiler of Sicily, has been indicted for theft, and Cicero must prosecute him. Toulouse is instructing fourteen year-old Dave about the Catalinian villainies.

Dave is just the most beautiful youngster anyone ever saw, small and dark, and a Black Irish diamond of adolescence. You know what I mean? He is not effeminate in any way, but Toulouse sits with him, his sacerdotal arm over Dave's shoulder. It wasn't pedophilia, just plain child exploitation.

By now most of us in '2A' are plain tired of Toulouse and his b.s. about the elite for Christ. In fact, I am relieved that he no longer comes over to the far corner of '2A' where I cower. He has lost interest in that corner of adolescent turmoil.

My own development during the rest of that year was sporadic. Toulouse seemed to have lost all interest in the class, in teaching, in any of us except Dave. But you daren't mess with Toulouse because he could cut you in a flash, and projected a physical menace on all of us, like a sultan ruling his harem.

An uncle of Dave Morse was Father Frank Duffey, S.J. Fr. Frank looked much like Davie and his older brother Jackie, short, very handsome, glowing with Catholic sexuality, and physically very tough. Several years later, when I was in the Jesuit Novitiate, Frank was one of my Latin teachers, and a very good one at that. He volunteered to me the information that his nephews were Jackie and Dave Morse.

I held my breath for a few seconds. It flashed on me that Fr. Duffey and Toulouse were classmates in the Jesuit Order. Both joined the Jesuits about 1934 or 1935. And both were from the same neighborhood in Spokane, a few blocks from the Caseys.

The message from Fr. Frank Duffey fixed itself into my noggin, and I asked myself, "Why is he telling me this; actually volunteering it?" Was he telling me some secret about Toulouse and Dave?

I kept mum, until many decades later, when one morning I looked at the headlines of the local paper, the Portland Oregonian, that the Jesuit Oregon Province (Oregon, Washington, Idaho, Montana, and Alaska) had declared bankruptcy because of lawsuits against it. All this stemmed from multitudinous pederasty and sacerdotal sodomy scandals, whose principle antagonist (dead for twenty-five to thirty years) was Fr. Michael Toulouse, S.J. I punched in the name "Jesuit pedophiles" on my Google machine, and, wouldn't you know, leading the list was Fr. Michael Toulouse, S.J., and Fr. Frank Duffey, S.J. This news came out ten years ago, and I am still disturbed by it all.

Remember, I saw and witnessed all of this, but only the surface of it.

In fact, there was far worse shit that happened. But what happened next did not occur until the first month of the following school year. Toulouse had a new crop of hearties in '2A'. I was now a junior, in the same '3A' elite class, but without a homeroom teacher.

After about a month of the school year 1950, my classmates start telling me that Toulouse is gone, not at Gonzaga High anymore. No one knows what, in fact, the deal is, but it is the talk of the school. In a day or so we hear that he has been transferred to Seattle University, to teach philosophy. This news comes to us against a background of, "Whoah! Very interesting." Much unknowing, and very much no one is talking.

I was now an upperclass junior, not directly affected by Toulouse's disappearance. But the episode hung in the air, like a silent but deadly fart, filling a sealed room. You could smell it, but the question was: who did it? Very adolescent gossip.

None of this actually blows over, it is just that no one speaks of it. You recall, that all of us in '2A' had seen Toulouse with his arm around Dave. Then Toulouse disappeared suddenly in the middle of the week. He has abandoned us, his elite, the very best among the soldiers of Christ. Did Toulouse leave or did he flee?

It is hard to believe that for fifty-five years, from 1950 to 2005, the facts were not only suppressed, but not even on record, outside of the Jesuit Archives in Portland, Oregon.

A giant lawsuit blew everything out into the open. And it was printed in the Oregonian and the Seattle Times.

What had happened in 1950 was that Toulouse was molesting some eleven year-old altar boy after his daily Mass at seven a.m. He did this in his room at the Jesuit residence. The newspaper gave the boy's name. It was not Dave Morse.

What happened next was the boy's own dad had asked him to go to Mass and communion with him. But the lad balked, then tried to hide from the dad. The dad pressed him until the lad spilled the beans.

Then the dad got his pistol, drove to the Jesuit residence, and marched into it like MacArthur back to Bataan. Some worthy Jesuit intercepted him, the pistol was pocketed, the police were called, and in less than an hour, Toulouse was at the train depot with a ticket to Seattle. Perhaps he was escorted by a detective.

By the way, Brothers and Sisters in Christ, what is your view of human nature, regarding pederasty? Toulouse was probably forty-five years old. Is it your opinion that this was his first go at the nasty stuff? Is that your view of human nature? "Yeah, sure."

"Your Honor, at the present time I am not able to say why the boy was in my cloistered room. Your Honor, please believe me. This just happened. Furthermore I have no recollection of any other event of this nature in my life. But, be assured, Your Honor, that this will never happen again. You have my word on this.

"And I trust that you will find in your heart the forgiveness I need so that I can carry on my ministry for the Kingdom of Christ.

"And I sincerely apologize to the boy and his family.

"Indeed, the provincial of the Oregon Province, Fr. Harold Small, S.J., will be writing a letter of gratitude to the Chief of the Spokane Police, on behalf of all my brother Jesuits, for keeping this matter quiet. May the Peace of Christ be with you."

So, why did the Spokane Police, and presumably the district attorney give Toulouse a pass? The Jesuits own much property in and around Spokane; and, Catholics vote in block.

Several years later, after I had joined the Jesuits myself, my mother visited me at the Novitiate. She asked me, "Well, why was Father Toulouse transferred out of town so quickly?" I muttered, "I dunno," because the concept of Toulouse as a pederast was not even within my imagination. Even so, my mother and other mothers of guys in the Jesuits were wondering about the Toulouse episode.

And I, like most other young Jesuits, was submerged in the boundless group-think of the 1950s.

I am often asked since the sacerdotal sodomy scandal broke open, "Gee, didn't you know? How could you not know?"

My answer is that owing to the ignorance of the 1940s and 1950s none of us could possibly know. Consciousness is not a computer; it is an excuse factory that prevents a person from making any hard decisions about who is lying to them. How else could Newt Gingrich get so many votes in an election?

The ones who did know (I mean really knew) were in the upper ranks, the power elite, the old boys network. This was the way the state and the Church worked. The groundlings scrubbed the floors, did the laundry, erased the blackboards, taught grammar, and coached freshman football.

Most of us groundlings did not know we were groundlings. We were just grateful to be on the team.

Toulouse became a big star in Seattle. He even developed his own T.V. program on the Fundamentals of Metaphysics; it was very popular; everyone spoke of it, how interesting it was, a blend of existentialism and Thomism. Can you imagine? I told you he was a brilliant talker.

One time, many years later (Toulouse died in 1976) I sat at a bar in the town of Havre, Montana. A woman about my age, sat across the way, and bragged about her years at Seattle University, "back in the fifties." I heard the word "Toulouse" sneak out of her mouth, and how he foretold that there would be future changes in the Catholic Church. I finished my beer and had to walk outside to get some fresh air. There is no end to Satan's Kingdom of Ignorance.

I was not finished with Toulouse's influence on me. After I was ordained a priest, I was assigned to teach philosophy at Seattle University. Toulouse still taught there. We were colleagues, not equals, but colleagues. In due course I will have more to say about him, pederasty, and my own development.

CHAPTER 4: MY MOTHER, TRUMAN, AND DEAN ATCHISON

After my sophomore year with Toulouse, I needed to scramble for a summer job to pay my tuition for the next year. I walked miles and miles in east Spokane where lumber mills and various railroad shops were in operation. I needed a work permit but state law stipulated that no employment was legal for young people under the age of sixteen. I was fifteen and I lied about my age. The trouble was that I looked like I was twelve. I applied to the Spokane City Parks Department. I filled out a form. There was no interview. Thus no one at City Hall saw that I looked only twelve. In a week, I got a phone call informing me that I'm hired, sight unseen, and am to report to Hillyard Swimming Pool as a locker boy.

The work there was easy. I handed out bags for kids to put their clothes in. I and another pseudo-sixteen year-old, Dick Olson, alternated between bags and sitting on a bench at the shallow end of the pool. We were supposed to watch over the little kids. No drowning was allowed.

The really good part was that there were two locker girls who sat with us. At last I got to talk with young females in bathing suits. God! I was thrilled. One of the locker girls, Jolene, had many friends, all female, who came to the pool everyday. They sat with Jolene, and of course, me, the perfect example of a confused adolescent. I was in the midst of cultural relativity, and, boy! did I love it. My natural adolescent clumsiness was exacerbated by the fact that these girls went to a public school and many were Protestants. The Church and Jesuits defined all these circumstances as an "occasion of sin." Did I have any chance at "normal" adolescent development? Also, the chief life guard often looked at me in a way that made me feel strange.

In the background of my Hillyard Swimming Pool experience was my mother's presence and her mindful concern for me.

Around the pool, girls in bathing suits were all over the place. Also there were guys there from the nearby John Rogers High. All they talked of was football season and beer parties. Thus, false impressions were implanted in my noggin.

What? you say, I haven't told you yet about that other Michael Casey, Oedipus Smeedypus? Well, golly, it's simple.

Oedipus Smeedypus is none other than the very mind of my mother, Margaret Grant Casey. Oedipus Smeedypus appeared in my life when I was a newborn Black Irish infant suckling at Mama's breast. As I suckled, Mama held her hand on the back of my head (I don't actually remember any of this, but I think it's true). My Achilles tendon stuck out the back of my head, and that son-of-a-gun Oedipus glommed onto it. The identification was complete. And ever since I have been a mama's boy. I am not a sissy or a fruit-nik. Yet I have always been a Mama's boy. And I was until she died in 1964. Whose boy I became after that is another story altogether.

A couple of the girls at the pool developed crushes on me and wanted me to come to their various parties. But I was a loyal Catholic smuck and lied my way out of the parties. I felt so disappointed in myself about this. I stayed locked in this smuck-like and retarded fear of women for many years.

You can see that it was easy for the Jesuits to recruit me.

My mother was an heroic figure. She held the Casey family together, four kids, and our father, Matt Casey, through very tight and often needy circumstances.

Mama was a hot lunch cook at some Catholic School. Our family lived from month to month on marginal paychecks. Both my parents felt they were lucky to have jobs.

My brother Dominic, now ten years old, had juvenile diabetes since his third birthday. Insulin injections were required three times a day. He could go into insulin shock at any time, and often did. Mama would give him one shot before she went to work, and rush home after cooking for other folks' kids to give him the next shot, then another after supper. Dominic often did not cooperate with this regime, and fought and screamed with all his might. Sometimes she didn't have the three dollars for a bottle of insulin, and had to ask me for the three bucks. I went to the drug store with my three dollars and bought the insulin. Concerning all of this, I plain shut my feelings off, and thought about the young girls at the Hillyard Swimming Pool. There was always hope.

Papa was a laborer He was over fifty years old, and you know what that meant for his employment prospects. He had been a farmer, a highway road worker, a coal miner, and a janitor at a small public school. All this was in North Dakota.

He is a good man but also a stubborn Irishman with fixed ideas about a man's place in the world. But now he is in Spokane, away from his exploitive family in Minnesota. He can't go back and he can't go forward.

And it shows on his face. He works nights at Phillips Petroleum refinery, and returns to our house at 904 East Indiana Street. He parks the Plymouth car and enters the house as all of us are about to leave, the kids to school, Patty to her job as a secretary downtown, and Mama headed to the bus stop to go to her job as a hot lunch cook somewhere in another parish.

Papa's face is ashen white. Christ Almighty, what is there in all this for him?

He is on the run from the Great Depression, from the failed farm in North Dakota. Roosevelt can't help him anymore, but he must fill the void, and earn money to feed us. The Church offers comfort, but no actual relief for the family. Matt is very tough, this Irishman is, but his religion is all take and no give. Remember this about the Jesuits, all take and no give.

He turns to religion and attends the eight-thirty Mass every weekday at St. Al's. On Saturday and Sunday the whole family goes to Mass and Communion. God Almighty Himself must be appeased and the Caseys are there at the Communion rail with the appeasement incense and cash offering; maybe we even light a cheezie candle to Saint Joseph, the patron saint of workers.

After Sunday Mass, Papa drives us home for a breakfast of oatmeal with brown sugar and milk. Then he gets into the Plymouth and returns to St. Al's to usher at the ten and eleven-thirty Masses. He is filling the void. In fact, the Caseys are just doomed to Catholic servitude. The nails that crucified Christ Himself have been pulled out of his body and driven into the hands and feet of Matt Casey, and thus into the entire Casey family.

In Spokane, the Caseys are just strangled by the ever-present Jesuits.

These sunken-cheeked pig-fuckers want everything, and in time they will get it.

Only our mother points us to what is valuable, education. Even if it is Catholic, it still is education.

During my freshman and sophomore years, my best friend was Jim Mahoney, a big Irish kid who had hundreds of dirty jokes and stories. This was food for a famished Oedipus Smeedypus lad from North Dakota.

Several guys in the neighborhood a few years older than Jim and Mike went to National Guard meetings on Wednesday nights at Fort George Wright. This was an ancient military base on the outskirts of Spokane. Jim said, "Come on, Meathead, let's go. My brother Dan and Joe, the Plumber, will be there. They can show us the ropes."

We went and attended several meetings in the next few months. Sixteen year-old adolescents marched around an indoor gymnasium holding wooden rifles from World War II.

Each marching kid received five dollars for each session. In the summer, each would get full pay during the four-week training session at the Yakima Firing Range. Some of these kids were smaller than I; and I was small.

A big sergeant in front of the group tells all present that when those fifteen year-olds sitting and watching from the side of the gymnasium turn sixteen, they too can march and get the five dollars a session. Boy! did this ever sound good to me.

After a couple of meetings, I returned to the Casey house and explained to Mama the wonder and allure of the five dollars per National Guard session. Five dollars is what I could earn in an entire week delivering the Spokane Chronicle. Mama erupted in fury and disgust. She began to holler at me as to what a meat-head I was. She stood up from the table, grabbed a broom from the corner of the kitchen, and began to wail away on me. The blows did not hurt but she made her point. She had got her family this far from the thistles of North Dakota, and, by God, marginal as we were in Spokane, Uncle Sam was not going to get his mitts on her prize lad enrolled in Gonzaga High School under the tutelage of Toulouse, the pederast.

In fact, I never went to another National Guard meeting.

This happened in March 1950. In June 1950, two months later, North Korea invaded South Korea, and the lads in Washington State National Guard were activated. I soon got the bribe of five dollars a day in perspective, and lost interest in marching.

The Korean War was nasty, and Mama's intelligent reaction, before the actual event, saved me from the carnage.

During the next two years at Gonzaga High, I never heard a single discussion about the Korean War. In the Jesuit curriculum the Korean War did not exist. Loyola's knights were simply not going over to Korea. The war was for the likes of Dan Mahoney and his friend Joe the Plumber, and other drop-outs. Loyola's special lads in the '2A' class were told to aspire to greater glory than a trench in Korea.

I want you to consider how my mother, before the event, had sized up the opposition to her children's education. Even the Jesuits were not as dangerous as Uncle Sam and Dean Atchison and Harry Truman.

I say this unto you, O Catholic Lads, listen to your mama and you just might survive the current or next war.

You know, don't you, about the passage in the Bible that says: "The Lord God sayeth: 'Give me a skinny small-boned fifteen year-old longing for the flesh-pots of the Hillyard Swimming Pool, and a fierce mother from North Dakota, and in no time at all, I will own an obedient Jesuit.'" God said that. Yes he did. It's in the Bible.

CHAPTER 5: UNION SCALE

As a sophomore I wanted to play basketball. I turned out for the sophomore Junior Varsity. So did everyone else. In two practices the coach cut seventy sophomores to ten. That was it for my athletic career.

The director of athletics was Father Harry Jahn, S.J. I asked him if I could be the property manager of the baseball team. He said "yes." I thought it was a good deal. I managed both the Junior Varsity, the Senior Varsity Baseball, and also the entire track team. About one hundred fifty athletes were involved. I had to be efficient and watchful at the same time. The guys were always trying to steal jerseys, socks, jock-straps, and towels. I kept a tight rein on it all. Father Jahn came to trust me, and even liked me. I also swept out the locker room floor after practice.

At the end of the season I received a varsity letter, the big 'G', with the word 'manager' printed on it. Thus I was allowed to join the Letterman's Club, and have my picture taken with the school's mighty jocks.

I liked Father Jahn so much and he relied on me so much, that I asked him if I could be the football and basketball manager for my junior year.

What was I thinking? I didn't understand what I was doing, but I really wanted to be "in." I had a distinct anti-elite complex but at the same time I wanted to be on a Gonzaga team. I reached for some small status despite my lack of athletic ability and total lack of talent for the school's debate and elocution teams, Gonzaga High's other big status symbols.

Well, I liked to work and keep busy. This made it easier for me to accept my bottom-level status at Gonzaga High School. Property managers, in an all boys' school devoted to Latin and football, get little respect.

In my junior year I managed the football and basketball teams. This went O.K. It kept me out of trouble. But also, it got me used to working for the Jesuits, for nothing. Working for nothing is not a wholesome long-term attitude to develop. I was taking small steps to joining the Jesuits even though I was unaware of my direction.

My best friend by this time was Phil Thompson. He lived only a block away from me, and we walked to school together. What I liked about him was that he read books, even better books than I read. Talking with him was always a pleasure. He had ideas and was interesting.

Phil was a very strong and fast athlete, and eventually was an All-State football player. His picture was in the papers. Since I was not athletic, there was no competition between us. Also, like me, he was terrified of women. We didn't have to compete with other guys for girlfriends.

The way things were going for both of us indicated that we were destined to join the Jesuits. What saved Phil from this calamity was the fact that his mother, a very devout woman, did not trust the Jesuits. The Jesuits were strong about recruiting Phil. He would be a big prize. His mother, however, shut this mad hysteria down and plucked Phil from the perdition that awaited me.

Another friend, Armand DeFelice, also an athlete and on a strong academic track, asked me if I wanted to work after school at his family's American Macaroni Manufacturing Company.

Armand, Phil, and Mike packed macaroni in a warehouse near downtown Spokane. The minimum wage then was seventy-five cents an hour. This was enough for milkshakes, Twinkies, and movies on weekends. My mother could see that I was hanging with a good crowd. This smoothed things out on the home front for me and her, since without the macaroni money, there would be no movies or milkshakes. Without these adolescent requirements I soon would be attending National Guard meetings for the despicable five dollars a night marching for Truman and Dean Atchison.

My junior year ended and I was desperate for a job, to get some money coming in, if only to pay my tuition for the next year.

I got wind from Phil, his friend Bill Kerley, and his friend Skip Hunting about employment prospects for the summer. This was 1951. Skip's girlfriend was the daughter of a big-ass paint contractor named Charles Stapleton. He had a contract to paint railroad bridges on the S. P. & S. railroad. (Spokane, Portland, and Seattle.) We all met at Stapleton's house one night in early June. I went along as a hopeful wet-back. Skip and Bill had graduated from Gonzaga High in May. Skip had a scholarship in football at Santa Clara University in California.

We sat down in Stapleton's front room after his supper. He explained the deal. He knew Skip and Bill and Phil. Me? The football manager? Huh? I hovered in the shadows. I was excited, the pay was two dollars and fifty cents an hour, union scale. It would be ten hours a day, six days a week.

He emphasized that there would be no overtime, and no per diem, and no reporting to the Iron Workers Union. He said it was a Communist outfit. The Iron Workers Union had jurisdiction over everything iron. This meant railroad bridges.

Every time he said two dollars and fifty cents an hour, my heart skipped a beat. Jesus! Has my day come for the big score? Stapleton emphasized that the hiring had to be O.K. with our families. But only two of us in the room would be hired, and had to be over eighteen years of age. My heart briefly sank, but I thought, "Well, I'll just lie about my age." I was sixteen and still looked twelve. I wanted the job. How? How?

The next night the four of us gathered in Skip Hunting's backyard: Bill was in for the deal, Phil had other plans, Skip had to convince his mother to let him go. He was eighteen but his mother didn't see it that way. "You already have a full scholarship to Santa Clara in the fall. I don't want you leaving us for the summer." Skip pleaded but she said, "No, Skip! You're not going." Stapleton had given two railroad passes (a free ticket courtesy of the S. P. and S.) to Bill and Skip. Skip was standing and pleading, holding the pass (ticket) in his hand. He said, "But Mr. Stapleton already has given me a pass." Mrs. Hunting said, "No Skip! You're staying home for the summer." Skip was almost bawling. Mike Casey, the ever-faithless scavenger of railroad passes, stood up next to Skip, and plucked the pass from his forlorn fingers, and said, "Mrs. Hunting, I'll take Skip's place and Mr. Stapleton's offer will be put to good use. It would be good for everyone if Skip stayed home with you for the summer. Please pray for Bill and me."

Was I that shameless? Damn right I was. Skip didn't need the job and I did. I never saw Skip again.

The next day Kerley and Casey were on the S. P. & S. train from Spokane to --- Washtucna, Washington. Don't bother searching

71

for the village on the map. It ceased to exist several decades ago. But Washtucna was in Palouse Country where there are endless grain fields and rolling prairie dry-gulching down to the Snake River.

Bill and I got off the train several miles from the village, and started walking. Bill had instructions on where we would stay. About eleven p.m. we got to Hotel Washtucna. There were no street lights. Two guys came out of Hotel Washtucna. They said, "We're Stapleton's crew and, come on, we got a room for you." This was spontaneous worker solidarity. And I am still amazed sixty years later at the cohesion of American workers on the individual level, looking out for each other.

We went upstairs, and in a small room, Bill and I saw the situation. There was a double bed against the wall. We put our bags down, took off our clothes, and crawled into the double. I was the junior partner and took the spot next to the wall. To get up I had to crawl over Kerley. There was also a small table and a chair.

Our lives as sweaty and steaming proletariats had begun.

The next morning, Stapleton's crew, Jake and Jack, woke us up at six a.m. and it was downstairs for breakfast at Cafe Washtucna. A matronly and heavy woman served up and made all four of us roast beef sandwiches that we could take to the job site. We paid for the breakfast and the lunches, stepped outside, and then crawled into a panel wagon driven by the foreman, Emmett McKinley. Now there are five of us. The thing is: McKinley thinks I'm Skip Hunting. I tell him, "I'm Mike Casey." He says, "Well there must be a mix-up."

I'm already in the panel wagon. Who I am doesn't seem to bother Emmett. However, I didn't know if I was actually on the crew until that weekend when I got my first paycheck.

Twenty miles south of Washtucna is the Snake River. Many ravines and coulees ran perpendicular to the Snake. Across these ravines were railroad trestles. These were about a hundred to a hundred and fifty feet tall. They needed cleaning and painting. Which is why Mike, Bill, Jake, and Jack were hired.

Emmett drove the panel wagon to a railroad siding. We got out and walked the two miles to the S. P. and S. trestle. The dry gulch under the trestle was the home of unfriendly rattlesnakes. I said a Hail Mary. We clamber down the gulch to the foot of a trestle tower, start the cleaning of it with wire brushes, and hammering on the rust corrosion on the towers.

It's a lot of fun. I wish each and every one of you could have this experience. Jake and Jack are sprayers. Bill and Mike are cleaners. There are no protocols. We just work like mad in the scorching sun. There is a half-hour lunch break. Then back to work. From eight a.m. to six p.m., ten hours, six days a week. Two dollars and fifty cents an hour.

At the end of the day, there's the drive back to Hotel Washtucna, all three rooms of it. One bathtub for four guys. I am fast and get in there first. Jack did not ever bathe; Kerley every so often, Jake usually. Cleaning bridges is very dirty work.

Then it's downstairs to Cafe Washtucna, and the nice supper of fried steak, potatoes, apple pie, and a glass of milk.

Here is how the line-up went: Emmett McKinley was experienced, had a fairly good education, and kept the peace between Jack and Jake, the sprayers. Jack was probably illiterate but a strong worker. Jake was an even stronger worker, and had no use for Jack. Bill Kerley was a good worker but just could not stand Jack and Jake. (Bill's father was a lawyer, and Bill inevitably had middle class aspirations.) Mike could just barely cut the mustard, but tried as hard as he could. He wanted to earn a man's wages. This was all there was for him. Kerley left the job in the middle of the summer. It wasn't the work; it was the guys (including me, whom he had to sleep with, farts and all).

This trestle took about two or three weeks to finish. So, where does Stapleton's crew go next?

Mr. Stapleton visits the job site one day in order to see if it will pass inspection. It does. He says to me, "You're not eighteen, are you?" His voice is not hostile but I have put him in potential trouble. (Washington State was a very strong union State and child labor laws were enforced.)

"You could get me in trouble, you know."

I say, "Yes, Mr. Stapleton, but I really want to work here." In fact, I was only sixteen. I say, "In a few weeks' time I'll be seventeen."

"O.K.," he says. Then, "You can go with the crew to Portland for the job there across the Willamette."

Like that, I'm in, and earn union scale.

For me, this is good luck. For my mother, this is Providence. In time I would see it her way.

Jake (I never actually knew his last name) seemed to take me under his wing. Jake, Kerley, and Casey got in Jake's 1948 Buick Sedan and head to Portland, Oregon where the next job awaits us. It's the railroad bridge across the Willamette River.

We arrive at Broadway and Burnside and rent rooms at the Burnside Hotel. It's still Casey and Kerley in one room and one bed. Jake has his own room. In the morning he drives us to the job site.

The site is close to the mouth of the Willamette where it flows into the Columbia. Cargo ships move up and down the river all day long. Passenger and freight trains roar past us five and six times a day.

The conditions are quite dangerous and there can be no dinkin' around on the bridge. You're up high, sixty feet above the track, scraping rust. Emmett McKinley knows when the trains are coming (that's why he is the foreman). The bridge is built to flex, up and down, as much as ten inches, to absorb the impact of the pounding wheels of the trains. Emmett hollers, "Hang tight." That means a train is coming. You stop work, secure your tools and paint can of red-lead primer, and ride out the Battle of D-Day on the Willamette. You can't relax and always need to pay careful attention.

The bridge is on high stone pillars secured to the bottom of the river. Now it's time to crawl down under the track to these pillars. The crew stretches two steel cables from one pillar to the next. A plank is fitted on these cables. The plank on the cables, Casey on the plank, the river below. You get the picture? I get on the plank and begin to clean and scrape the flanges on the girders. These are rusty in spots, layered over with pigeon shit nearly all way, and worst of all, much toilet paper and human fecal matter. Were you aware that the passenger trains flush their toilets as they race over the bridge? Casey and Kerley must wear caps since it does happen that occasionally there is a direct hit on the cleaners below. One morning the wind blew Kerley's cap into the river. That afternoon after lunch, the improbable direct hit occurs. When payday came on Saturday, Kerley told the foreman that he was quitting and got on the train back to Spokane.

My close call came later, but it wasn't a fecal hit. I was riding a plank on the cables, pulling myself along from pillar to pillar. To do this, I step off the plank onto the cables, then use my other foot to nudge the plank along a foot or so. This was standard procedure. A long flat wheeler came along. (A flat wheeler is a box car whose four wheels are no longer circular, but ground flat from constant and prolonged braking. The wheels are more like octagons). All goes ok, until about four or five or six flat-wheelers are strung together. Now, the laws of physics take over. The pounding on the track above is ferocious. The plank and the cables are waving up and down like a ferris-wheel. I grew apprehensive and decided to step off the plank with both feet on the cable and then just hang on to the flange of the girder for balance. I did this. The plank waved good-bye and plunged into the Willamette. Then I eased my way up along the cables to the stone pillar inch by inch. At least the pillars weren't moving. I was regaining my composure when Emmett looked down at me and said, "Mike, now we have to get you another plank."

What he said, understated, was a vote of confidence in me as a man. No scolding or emotional outburst. He treated me like a man. And therefore I was a man.

Every week the crew was paid. I kept enough of my check to pay for my hotel room, and for meals at Pat's Bar and Grill in the St. John's district of Portland. The rest I sent to my mother (Oedipus, Schmeedipus!).

A woman named Pat owned the grill and made fabulous breakfasts and lunches for me and the others. She ignored the "Minors Not Allowed" sign on her own bar and grill door. Pat wanted me to date one of her daughters (she had several). My work mates, guys thirty years older than I, were poking me in the ribs, and whispering,

"Go for it, dumb-bell." But I was gutless about women. Besides, I really dug Pat herself, a shapely and charming woman of forty years who had worked in a bar and grill all her life. But again, Oedipus Smeedypus! intervened, and on Sundays I went to Mass instead. Jerk! What's wrong with you?

Actually, there was nothing wrong with me. I was a skinny sixteen year old, striving to earn a man's wages. My mother had put all her trust and hopes in me. I didn't want to disappoint her or my family. It was family honor.

By now, I was seventeen, and it was family honor versus Pat and her comely daughters.

The guys on the crew took me under their wing, and coached me on how to avoid dangerous situations, like getting run over by an unscheduled freight train. I learned to work with other older guys, and earned their respect.

After work (ten hours a day, and six days a week) I returned to the working man's hotel in St. Johns, a suburb of Portland. The rent was seven dollars a week, with a common bath. I cleaned up, scraped off the day's grime and dirt, put on clean clothes, went to a restaurant nearby. Jake always came with me. The place had rib eye steaks for seventy-five cents apiece. I always ordered two steaks. It came with spuds, gravy, green beans, apple pie and ice cream. Then I returned to my seven dollars a week room, listened to my radio for a while (Lucky Lager, Top Forty), and fell asleep. This went on for several months.

On Saturday night, St. John's was alive and noisy until well past midnight. Workers cashed their paychecks and started drinking. This included several guys on the Stapleton painting crew. Most of these workers lived on the same floor where I slept. They crawled back to their rooms at one and two P.M.

One guy in particular, Jack Thompson, had the room next to mine. His wife lived there with him. He had told me that he had been married three times and his wife nine times. I looked at his wife and believed him.

One Saturday night or Sunday morning, I awoke to the sound of Jack Thompson beating his wife. "Slap, slap, punch, punch" it went. His voice, angry and slurred with booze, kept saying, "Goddam, you'll never embarrass me again." Then it was more "slap, slap," and "punch, punch," while his wife groaned and gasped. Jack's slurred talk was barely understandable.

In the middle of a hot summer night in St. John's, a suburb of Portland on the Willamette River, this crucifixion took place, and I heard it. Over sixty years later I can still hear Jack's voice and the sound of his slaps and his wife's groaning. There was no question of me intervening. Jack was tall and had a powerful physique. I was a scrawny sixteen year old, sleepy and tired and his door was locked.

But I was deeply affected by this. For me, this was an experience of evil. And I could tell no one of it. And I never did. But, nevertheless, it gestated inside me.

It is easy for some folk, years after the fact, to say that I should have leapt out of bed and defended the woman, or stopped Jack's fists. But that is an illusion. Moral evil is not a discrete commodity one individual can rectify. My experience was that I could only bear it, and possibly learn from it, for my own benefit.

The event entered into me. And, a year later when I considered joining the Jesuits, i.e., leaving the world and all its muck and groaning, I just knew that I wanted a haven from the likes of Jack Thompson and painting railroad bridges, and the lost souls of the hotel in St. John's.

The Jesuit noose around my neck was getting tight. The Jesuits were pulling in one direction, with encouragement from my mother.

Pulling in the other direction was Pat at her Bar and Grill, and her daughters.

Apparently what I really needed was the stability of the Jesuit Order.

I finished my stint on the Willamette and returned to Spokane. I didn't want to, but family pressure prevailed. I began my senior year at Gonzaga High in September, 1951.

CHAPTER 6: CONGRATULATIONS: YOU'RE IN

After four years at Gonzaga High School, it never occurred to me that I had a choice about joining the Jesuits. For me, there was no weighing of the pros and cons. A few months before graduation, Father Toner, S.J., the principal of the school (whom I really admired) asked me if I wanted to join the Jesuits.

I had been getting warm to the idea for some months. I said, "O.K., I'll go to Sheridan." (Sheridan, Oregon was the location of the Jesuit Novitiate.)

My mother did not outright pressure me, but she kept bringing up the subject, saying, "I think it's a really good idea." Remember that she was the one who pulled us all out of North Dakota in 1948 so that all of us kids could get a Catholic education.

But the clincher for the Sheridan trip was from Father Jerry Murray, S.J., our mathematics teacher. In March he was scheduled to preach the Novena of Grace in St. Al's church. Hundreds of people came to this every year and it meant more to him than teaching mathematics. Murray told me that in his absence I was to teach the class in mathematics. He would be gone for nine days. At first I thought he was kidding. But Father Toner assured me that this was the real deal. So, I did it. Like an actual Jesuit, I had no choice.

For nine days, I boogied to the differential equations. I wasn't a great mathematician, but I could teach. This is how the Jesuits recruited me.

A Jesuit takes vows of poverty, chastity, and obedience. Let me explain my adolescent understanding of this.

Chastity was no problem for me since I knew no girls (i.e. women) and was terrified of even speaking to them (Gonzaga High was an all-male school. Even the University had only gone co-ed just a couple of years before.) When I heard of someone getting married, I simply shrunk within myself at the thought of such a fate for me. I liked girls in the neighborhood, but as soon as talking to them was required, I hid behind the nearest bush.

My mother always wanted me to join the Jesuits, and our Freudian friend, Oedipus Smeedypus, steered me away from any conversation with young women. After all, my mother might be listening.

I was seventeen and the vow of chastity was not an issue for me, until ten years later when it became the only issue for me. But that was then.

The vow of obedience also was not then an issue since I had worked in factories and on construction crews. To me, obedience was simply doing what your boss told you to do.

But the real kicker for me was the vow of poverty. This vow means that you must divest yourself of all worldly goods. When you enter the Order, you do so without anything in your name. When I joined the Jesuits, I was required to relinquish everything I owned. I mean everything.

Well, what did I own? I owned a 1936 Plymouth. I paid one hundred fifty dollars for it. I had repaired this car with new piston rings and well-ground valves. It was not a hot car, but it moved nice. I had painted it a metallic maroon. My buddies and I toured the city of Spokane nearly every night, honking the horn at any woman standing at a bus stop. I did not bother asking Fr. Toner if I could take my 1936 Plymouth with me to the Jesuit Novitiate.

Not many seventeen year-olds in 1952 had automobiles. But I did, and hated to give it away.

But the really big possession I held was a $2,000 scholarship from Phillips Petroleum. I have already told you about this. It could be applied to any school of my choice. The scholarship was doled out at the rate of five hundred dollars a year. In 1952, this was equivalent to a year's tuition, fees, and books to a top university, like the University of Washington. The tuition was not specific to any school, and the checks were written to me personally.

This scholarship was my real inheritance from my father, Matt Casey, and from my family. As you read this, you're thinking, what's the big deal about a two thousand dollar scholarship in 1952?

You're thinking this, aren't you? But was your mother a hot lunch cook in a parish school? Was your father a janitor at Phillips Refinery in Spokane? Was your brother Dominic weakening daily from infantile diabetes? Did my parents' two paychecks sustain the cost of insulin and the weekly grocery bill and utilities?

Tight, Bro, very tight, and I am not yet, sixty years later, reconciled to the tight, very tight squeezing of the Casey household.

Here's how to think of what a $2,000 scholarship was actually worth. What, today, is a four year college diploma worth, minus board and room? At state schools it can go $15,000 to $20,000 a year in tuition and fees. Certainly, times and numbers change, but I'm talking what that scholarship was actually worth in 1952.

MICHAEL M. CASEY
Son of M. R. Casey,
Warehouseman, Refining,
Spokane, Washington

Figure 7 Scholarship Photo, 1952

And then I signed it away to the Jesuits, the richest religious order in the Catholic Church. What perversion of values had taken place in the Casey family? The perversion was that the Casey family were merely serfs in the Jesuit Kingdom.

A guy marries the Jesuits, and the Jesuits get rich. This is the vow of poverty.

After graduation I went back to work for Stapleton on a new bridge-job over the Columbia River at Vancouver. I was living in a cheap hotel there, listening on my radio to Kasey Kasem's Top Forty Lucky Lager's Hits, when I received a letter from the Jesuit High Command that I was accepted as a Novice into the Jesuit Order, Oregon Province. The letter said, "Congratulations, you're in. Here's a list of clothes you must bring with you. Also, be at the Novitiate in Sheridan, Oregon on August 15th, the Feast of the Assumption of our Lady Mary into heaven." At the time I was dreaming about Pat of Pat's Bar and Grill, and her two daughters.

The next day I told my boss Emmett that I was returning to Spokane. He was disappointed but I went anyway.

On July 7th I turned eighteen and went to work at Kaiser Aluminum's plant in Mead, Washington. I worked on the "pot" line. The conditions were certainly the worst I ever sweated under.

Bauxite ore is the stuff that is the source of aluminum. A pot line is a row of electrically charged iron rods with a large carbon "football" sized base. A molten "pot" is beneath this, and, a pot man, me, pulls a lever, and the bauxite ore falls down on the furnace of molten aluminum. The pot man used a long, heavy iron poker to break up the molten bauxite. A guy can hardly breathe. Dante had no idea how hot this is: it is hell itself. Nothing like bauxite dust to confirm in me the idea that I had a vocation to the Jesuits.

But the pay was good. I worked there for a month, banking all my money.

On August 12th, as doom's day approached, I quit Kaiser and drove off in my car to a bank near the Casey house. I cashed my last paycheck and withdrew all of my money, about a thousand dollars, put it into a brown paper grocery sack, and gave it to my mother. I didn't know how else to handle my affairs.

Since graduation, a couple of months before, I had been buddies with a classmate, Jim Herlihy. He was the class valedictorian and was also going to Sheridan. He and I agreed to meet at the Great Northern depot in downtown Spokane. After supper on the appointed day, Mama, Papa, and Michael get into my Plymouth and I drive it to the depot. The Herlihy family is already there. Inside the depot I handed the title and the keys to my Plymouth to Papa. I told him the gas-tank was full.

The Caseys and the Herlihys are both survivors of the Great Depression and thus there will be no hugs or goodbye kisses.

We all said goodbye. Jim and I lifted our bags and got on the train. Mama and Papa, and Mr. and Mrs. Herlihy stood at the gates and waved to us. Jim and Mike found seats on the train, sat and pondered what they had done. Then the train left the station and we fell asleep.

CHAPTER 7: FROM SPOKANE TO THE BEDWETTER FOR HITLER

The S. P. & S. train just kept moving on: Spokane, Yakima, Pasco, Wishram, Washougal, Vancouver, and across the very bridge over the Columbia I had painted just a month earlier, and at last to Portland. Herlihy and Casey both talk about women and how great it would be if we could just meet a couple of women our age. Actually we did not say "women" but "girls". Alas, these women are not on the train. But what else was there to talk about? Two eighteen year-old guys (boys, really) were drawn to the Jesuit Order, a religious group of celibate reactionaries who abhorred all women, regardless of age.

We were not lost or demented, but merely confused. We believed that we could live a life of Poverty, Chastity, and Obedience. We were not dumb-dumbs or stupid, but very idealistic. We were not avoiding growing up. I, at least, wanted a place to land, to become educated, to realize my family's faith in me. Painting railroad bridges or working "pot line" would not do this for me. But, I believed that joining the Jesuits would. And the Jesuits told me it was possible.

Is it so awful to be so idealistic, even if years later I became aware of the Jesuit iniquity, dishonesty, and duplicity? No, it is not awful. But it can lead to devastating disillusionment, if in the course of time and events, when Mike Casey at last realized that the Jesuit Order and the Church itself was all bullshit. Really, all bullshit. But that was years in the future.

And always remember that Mike Casey was a hardworking but simple Irish soul. It just never occurs to him to ask any questions about what life in the Jesuits would be like. I simply accepted my fate back in Spokane about what I was getting into when I volunteered as a soldier in Loyola's Army.

Herlihy and Casey transfer from the train depot in Portland to the Greyhound Depot for a bus to Sheridan, Oregon, about fifty miles southwest in the Yamhill Valley. At Sheridan, we get off the bus, hold our bags in one hand until a driver pulls up to the curb. He says who he is, tells us to put our bags into the trunk. The temperature is 100 degrees. We crawl into the 1946 Chevy two door. We begin a drive up a high hill that overlooks the Yamhill Valley and the Yamhill River. At the top of the hill is the Novitiate of St. Francis Xavier. Half-way up the hill the driver, who has introduced himself as John Swartze, from Spokane, shifts the Chevy into second gear, so steep is the hill. Finally, we reach the top, and pull in front of the main, and virtually only building.

The building of the Novitiate was a four story cement edifice, covered not with brick or stucco, but with black tar. Short wire rebar stuck out from the surface every two feet. It had Stalin and Mussolini written all over it.

We got out of the car and grabbed our bags. Then we stepped up to the front entrance of St. Francis Xavier Novitiate. We wonder what's next?

Then a very tall and skinny black robe steps out of the shadows and acknowledges our existence. He is Father Master, the Master of the novices. The greeting does not allow for critical questioning. Someone whispers that he is Jesus Christ Himself. He says shit and we all squat. But this man never has to say such crude formulae. His demeanor and physical stature alone command our respect. His real name is William Elliot. But to us novices, he was, and always will be, Father Master.

He is about six-feet-three and very skinny. His legs are long and his torso short, his buns seem to be up near his shoulder blades. But his eyes are like search lights from a guard tower. Nothing escapes them. Not even Houdini could untie himself if Father Master was watching. If you pass the test of his eyes, you are in the Jesuit Order. If his eyes blink at you, you are down the steep hill to Sheridan and hitchhiking to Spokane.

O.K., here's the deal about Father Elliott, or Father Master:

As time went on in the Novitiate, I came to realize that Father Master was what stabilized me as a Jesuit. The pious thought that I would be serving God "Ad majoram Dei Gloriam" never grabbed me. But Father Master's presence did. It never occurred to me to analyze him or to talk about him to other novices. My feelings were not personal, nor were his. He did not give pep talks, ever. Yet he was an excellent speaker. Ferverinos were not his style. I wanted to be a Jesuit, and here he was, as close to a soldier of Loyola as was possible.

All subsequent superiors I had in the Jesuits were not of his caliber at all. They were hacks or bullies or bullshitters, or all three.

What quality he had that others did not, well, I'm just not capable of stating. But he had it; that's just how it was.

In high school, of the Jesuits I knew, some were good guys (Father Jahn, Father Toner), others were boring or dull. Some were terrific teachers, Mr. Schlatter, especially (Latin and Greek) and Father Jerry Murrey. But Father Master, without any pep talks or "counseling" set a standard which I thought was the purpose of joining the Order.

Father Elliott is neither grim nor jolly. He is Father Master, absolutely in control of himself. And this indicates that you too must always be in control of yourself. The scene is like General George Patton looking over his troops, before battle. He is not especially authoritarian. Yet he is very serious. His presence indicates what is expected of you. He owes none of us anything, but he is also not arrogant.

Only once, as I will show you shortly, did he ever betray any prejudice against a person (me!) in favor of the Jesuit Order itself. It was an unworthy betrayal but one that left its mark on me for many years.

After a bit, other novices began to arrive. The class of 1952 eventually was comprised of about thirty idealistic eighteen to twenty year olds. Also there were a number of older guys who had even been in World War II. One older man, John McBride, had just recently been discharged from the Army having suffered some wounds in the Korean War. He walked with a bit of a limp. These older guys were a good stabilizing influence on the group. And they told no war stories. A few of our class were college graduates, many had two years of college, age about twenty, and now eligible for the draft for the Korean War, and thinking that seminary deferment (4F) looks really good. The rest of us were just out of high school. Some, like me, didn't even have to shave every day.

Shortly we are all shown to our "cubicles". Each wing of the place had five or six long rooms. Think of these rooms as forty feet long and twelve feet wide rectangles. A single door admits the Jesuit livestock into twelve stalls (the number twelve suggests the twelve apostles and a horse or mule for each apostle, but I am only imagining this).

An aisle ran the length of the room, wide enough for one person to walk. The walls of each cubicle are seven feet tall, running to about three feet from the ceiling. A heavy brown canvas curtain hangs at the front edge of each cubicle. These walls are unpainted wood. They look and smell like old burlap potato sacks. Opposite each cubicle is a window through which the prisoner (excuse me, the Novice) can gaze out and behold the Yamhill River in the valley below. But you're not supposed to look out the window, lest you develop thoughts of escape.

Each cubicle had a table, a small stand with shelves for your clothing, a kneeler, and a chair that squeaked. The desk had a crucifix hanging above it. There were no pictures on the walls. On each desk was a copy of Thomas à Kempis' Imitation of Christ, a Webster's 2nd Collegiate Dictionary (my salvation), a Cassell's Latin / English Dictionary, and a large book called Spiritual Reading, written by some Jesuit lunatic named Alphonsis Rodriguez. It was written about the time of Queen Isabella of Spain in the sixteenth century.

A novice was assigned to a cubicle for four months, after which everyone would be moved around. For four years no one was allowed to choose his own cubicle or his neighbors. Replace the canvas curtain with iron bars and you have a prison. Replace Thomas à Kempis with Mein Kampf and you have a Nazi prison. Replace Rodriguez's

Spiritual Reading with the Communist Manifesto and you have Stalin's Lubianka. Altogether it's a Jesuit Novitiate. And never underestimate how much repressive shit an idealistic eighteen year old can swallow.

Each dormitory of twelve cubicles had a room "beadle". A beadle is a minor official, appointed by Father Master, as cubicle enforcer and spy. Four times a day, during the two periods of meditation, and the two periods of examination of conscience, the room beadle walks the length of the room up and down the aisle by the window. He is checking to see if you are kneeling, not sitting, on your tiny kneeler, and certainly not lying down on your bed snoozing (obviously, my main character defect).

The cubicle beadle for my first four months was George St. Hilaire, N.S.J. (novice of the Society of Jesus). His name rhymes with George St. Hot Air. George, a true creep of Christ, was born for the job of cubicle spy and enforcer. I suspect that even Father Master couldn't stand him.

But wait, before you are designated a novice, you are first a Postulant of the Society of Jesus. This period lasts for twelve days. No demands are placed on you during the twelve days except that you must get up at five a.m. with everyone else, go to Mass, and eat your meals with the other postulants. You just stand at the door and wait for Father Master to open it, and hand you a used black cassock, a cincture, and a rosary about five feet long.

These twelve days of postulancy gave the local Father Master a chance to look you over. Maybe there's something about your health or character that was not discovered back in Spokane by Father Toner.

Years later I found out some curious information about a postulant who got the boot at the end of the twelve days, and then went on to become quite famous. His name was Martin Heidegger. Martin, a pious lad of seventeen years, had joined a German Province of the Jesuit Order. This was in 1906. Martin completed the twelve days of postulancy. The Novice Master thought it wise to send him home. Martin, you see, was a bed-wetter. This was intolerable in a religious order based on a common schedule (and think of the smell of pee when everyone awakes at five a.m. to begin meditating on the seven sorrowful mysteries). Thereafter Martin became a bed-wetter for Hitler. But I digress.

At the end of these twelve days you are given a cassock (the black robe), a cincture, an ostentatious five foot rosary which is to be worn over the cincture. All these articles are arranged with your name on a card in the large conference room. We all stand at attention and in silence. Father Master enters, says a Glory Be, and Ave Maria, a Pater Noster. He then blesses all the articles, and just like that, we are all Novices of the Order. And I liked it all.

Figure 8 1952: Novices: Herlicy, MacDonald, Casey

CHAPTER 8: THE RULES: THERE IS NO END TO THEM.

The make-or-break trial for a novice was the Long Retreat of Ignatius Loyola. It was thirty days of silence, penance, meditation, and a General Confession. It did not begin until September 30th, the feast of St. Michael the Archangel.

Let me digress (briefly!) about this famous Archangel. He was my patron saint. His wings were very wide and I felt secure that I was sheltered under them. In the last hundred years, the Catholic Church has virtually ceased to honor St. Michael. And that is why, actually, the Church has plain gone to hell.

Instead it honors dozens of ecclesiastical bureaucrats named Pius the This, Pius the That. Pius the Ninth was an imbecile, as was Pius the Tenth. Pius the Eleventh was pro-Hitler, but on his deathbed had a change of heart about the Fuhrer. When this was reported to

Eugenio Pacelli, the pope was driven in an open-top Cadillac through Dealy Plaza. R.I.P. for him. After Pacelli emerged from the sixth-floor of a nearby warehouse, he took the name Pius the Twelfth, became a Nazi diplomat and a big-time banker. And so far I haven't even mentioned that C.I.A. asset named John Paul le Duce. On these points you will have to do your own research.

But before I plunge you into the Long Retreat, or the Spiritual Exercises of Ignatius Loyola, there is much I must tell you about Jesuit boogerosity.

First, there are the rules. These were rules for all Jesuits, not just Jesuit Novices. These rules were written down in a book, a Rule Book. The Book was published in Loyola's lifetime. You had to know every one of them. And if you broke a rule, you were obliged to confess the infraction.

Most of these were rules of Modesty. There was Modesty of the eyes. You were not ever to move your head around to look at other novices, not even if the guy had a hare-lip. You are walking down the hallway, and a guy you knew for four years in high school, neither of you can make eye contact.

There were other rules of Modesty. Never, under any circumstances, were you to cross your legs – Christ Almighty, I really mean this – while sitting. Leg-crossing was called a major Arsinius (Arsinius was some ancient bishop who crossed his legs once and set off the French Revolution). Also there was a minor Arsinius. This was the mere crossing of your feet while sitting. (It was said that Masons and Atheists did this.) But the worst infraction of the rules of Modesty was walking around with your hands in your pockets. Of course, this might imply that you were a pervert and were playing with your nuts or dick. And there were other rules too numerous to mention. There was also the Rules of Title: Everyone was called "Brother". No first names were allowed. These rules built up barriers between you and your brother Jesuits. There was the rule of Grades. You could never talk to a priest at the Novitiate, except to Father Master or to the Latin or Greek teacher during class. You could not talk to any lay brother unless you were actually working for him, say, in the laundry, kitchen, or the farm. After a novice took vows, he was called a scholastic (that is, he is studying full-time and not "just" praying like a novice). Well, you could never even as much as say "hello" to a scholastic. Thus, Bob Tauksley, who lived exactly across the alley from the Casey household in Spokane, and who was two years ahead of me in the Jesuits, could walk past me in the hallway, and we would not even make eye contact. He was a scholastic and I a novice. And Herby MacDonald, whom I knew for four years in high school and who was my locker mate for one full year, had to call me "Brother Casey" and whom I had to call "Brother MacDonald," even while we were both working side by side in the alfalfa fields, picking up and heaving bales of the stuff high over our heads on to the truck. No exceptions. The sick part of all this is not that most of us abided by the rules, but we enforced these rules on each other. Very few of us were actually rats or snitches; peer group pressure worked hand in hand with Catholic Orthodoxy. Thus the Book of Rules always prevailed.

But the really big rule was against particular friendships. "Particular" here meant personal. I just could not understand this rule but I accepted it. I think I accepted it because I couldn't understand it. And no one, not even Father Master, could tell me what it meant. Strange and confusing.

At first I went to Father Master to ask him how I was supposed to deal with the fact that a number of novices I just plain did not like. He would say, "Brother Casey, you can't help your feelings, but you need to see Christ in them." Sometimes he would say, "Well, try to see some good in them." I never argued with him. Such was equivalent to blasphemy. I could see good in these guys. That wasn't the problem. I just plain did not like them. Some guys were creeps, some were arrogant. Many, I sensed, came from wealthy Republican families, a prejudice I could never overcome. And others were patronizing to Irish.

But the rule against particular friendships was not really about my prejudice against Republicans or Anglo-philes. It was something much more hidden in the shadows. It was a rule against two guys who grooved with each other to the exclusion of others. That is, they were fruits, fairies, or queers; maybe they were in love. This was in 1952, and I had never even heard the word "homosexual". And I had even been raped in a bunkhouse when I was thirteen years old. But that was not homosexuality. Rather, it was violence and chickenshit. There was no word current then for what happened to me. It never occurred to me that the rapist was a sexual deviant. I just thought he was a farm machinery salesman, who was also an ugly creep, and a danger to my life.

It is easy now, looking from the perspective of 2013, with decades of sexual openness and honesty, to be judgmental about attitudes in force in America in the 1940s and 1950s. But in 1952 most of the guys my age and experience (or lack of it) did not have a useful vocabulary to express what it was for males to like each other.

CHAPTER 9: GRAND SILENCE AND (GOOD GRIEF) THE SPECTOR OF HOMOSEXUALITY

Silence is the other big rule, maybe the very biggest. You wake up at five a.m., and there is no talking, not even while working in scullery or while waiting tables. This silence is in force until one p.m. when it's time for noon recreation. But it's not just silence in force; it's the suppression of any social nature for the cause of Loyola's Army.

And it was strict. And it was enforced by peer group pressure. If someone was jabbering in his cubicle, the room beadle would sprint down to Father Master's room and "report" this infraction.

A bell rings at the end of noon recreation (talking permitted, even demanded) and everyone stands; we all recite some group prayer, and then it's silence until two p.m. when some general work or play order begins. When the latter is completed, it's silence again until evening recreation from seven p.m., to seven forty-five p.m., and then Grand Silence until the next day at noon recreation.

And we are young American guys, full of testosterone and questions about American life, like the World Series, the Korean War, Stevenson versus Eisenhower, the Rosenberg Trial, Carl Perkins and his Blue Suede Shoes. Holy Fuck! What's wrong with us? It is not possible to give a rational answer to that question. The science of mind control, over Americans, was just beginning. (Are you aware that in 1952 Allen Dulles became head of the C.I.A., and was borrowing programs and techniques from the Nazis, who in turn borrowed them from Lenin and Stalin, all of whom admired Loyola's Army? The Grand Inquisitor was squirting his bile, centuries later, over the lads of the Oregon Province.)

Well, you get my drift.

And none of us were aware of this silent and invisible force of suppression of our natural vitality. We stuck our snouts into the trough and slurped it up.

And then, there's work. Work for the novices is assigned on a weekly basis: waiting on tables, reading at the main meal, scullery during the main meal, scullery after the main meal, setting the tables in the refectory, cleaning the toilets in the main building, cleaning the chapel where our Lord sits, utterly forlorn in the tabernacle. This is almost like when you are trapped in the crapper without toilet paper. Are you running with me, Jesus? All these are chores done in silence and with dispatch. We are being trained to be obedient Jesuits.

But the main bait set over the trap of Jesuit obedience is the evening recreation. In the Novitiate, "recreation" does not mean table tennis or pinochle. It means recreating your spirit by pious conversation.

Supper is over and the dishes are washed. The tables are set for tomorrow's breakfast. Now is the time for "recreation". It is the time for "recreating your spirit" by pious conversation to an assigned partner. You are to recreate your spirit by conversing about a book, say, you are reading, or about what Father Master had lectured on that morning. In other words, talking is allowed, even encouraged. But opinions are not.

You leave the chapel and are assigned your partner for that evening's recreation. Sometimes you get someone cool, like Dick Leach, my friend from high school who often had gossip or told jokes. Usually, however, it's some drudge from Idaho or Tacoma who wants to talk to you about the five Glorious or Joyful Mysteries, "And, aren't they just wonderful!"

However, once a week it's general recreation and no partners are assigned. You can talk to guys you can groove with.

This was when I got to be friends with Terry Corrigan. He was about three years older than I, probably the most intelligent guy in the class of 1952. He had spent his high school years at a minor seminary (ages 14 to 18) near Seattle. (A minor seminary is where young men for the diocesan priesthood are prepared. In fact, it is a cesspool of pedophiles on the make.) Then he switched to Seattle University, a Jesuit school where two of his uncles were Jesuit teachers. Terry was very articulate and had read much literature, qualities that I admired. He was very friendly to me. I liked him. And he was Irish.

After one of these recreation periods, all of us are filing back into the building. Terry sort of steers me to the side, and whispers, "Stay out here with me. I want to talk to you about something." I shake him off but he persists. What he is asking me to do is against all the rules of the Jesuit Order, which I have told you about. There could be no "particular" friendships and absolutely no talking during Grand Silence, which began at the end of recreation (about 7:30 p.m.) and lasted the next day until 1 p.m.

And of course I am a social prude. I shook him off again. I didn't want to have anything to do with this. Besides Terry had told me that when he was at Seattle University he had Father Michael Toulouse, S.J. as a philosophy teacher. This put me on guard even more. I was nervous about breaking out of the pack even for a few minutes to talk with him. I had resolved to make a go of this Jesuit thing and could not bear to have Father Master admonish me.

But Terry kept at it and I relented. We walked around the corner of the building and down a path behind some bushes where there was a bench. We sat down. Terry was shaking, almost trembling. What is going on with him?

He says, "Case, do you like me?"

Whoahh! This is not my game. I edge away a bit.

"I want to tell you that I'm really attracted to you." Then, he repeats this.

This is 1952. Guys like Terry were called "fairies", "fruits", or "queers". I had learned these words at Gonzaga High but had never met anyone who fit the definition. In fact, I had no idea of what all of this referred to. Remember my profession of sexual ignorance? On my part, this was deeper than ignorance. I could not comprehend that a guy would be attracted to me. I stare into the crystal ball, and no information comes up. It's just not there. In high school, a few girls my age had told me that they had crushes on me. But this just petrified me. I was not just a shy guy. I was a gold bar buried and locked six stories down at Fort Knox.

He says it again. "I am really attracted to you."

I can't remember what I finally said, but I manage a "Yeah, mmm...O.K." He was still trembling. I didn't give him an outright rejection, but I say, "I want to go inside. Don't tell Father Master about this."

He says, "Is this O.K., Case?"

I say, "Yeah, sure, it's O.K."

At this moment my life as a Jesuit hypocrite had begun: saying I was O.K. just to make people feel O.K. themselves, that you were not against them, continued for many years until I managed to split from the Jesuits altogether.

But, here's the irony: The rest of my time in the Jesuits, Terry Corrigan became my closest friend.

At that time I was not only a sexual prude, but a human prude. Is it a sin for one human to like another human?

Every time the Church says, "Sin!", it means that some folk are no good. And it took me years to realize that I should just give up the word 'sin' altogether. But that takes much education and experience. In the Novitiate, I did not have either.

In time I manage to get the idea of homosexuality figured out for myself (thanks to the aforementioned Oscar Mendez, S.J. in Toronto in 1962). But until that time the word "homosexuality" had to suffice, and maybe an occasional reference to "queer". Actually, the term Particular Friendships was more useful because of the fact that some guys were very tight with each other, and managed to exclude other guys from the conversations and activities. But this did not seem to be a sexual thing. For myself, I was O.K. with most of the guys I was with, while at the same time there were some guys I plain didn't like, and a number of guys that I naturally gravitated to because of mutual interests and tastes. But I never thought of myself as someone who had a particular friendship with anyone. In that regard, I was a pro-rule guy. I have always been an egalitarian (except for snots who don't like Irish, or any underdog for that matter). The phrase "particular friendship", so vague and vacuous, had to suffice for the time being. Remember, that Father Master himself could not clarify it for me.

If the explanation I have presented here is confusing, I beg you to appreciate that both the human and sexual issues are confusing. No one is born just plain knowing how it all goes. Some folk do get it figured out, or come to terms with it. And others don't. But when the Church (Pius the This, Pius the That) pontificates on it all, or sprinkles hoodle-dust over natural sexual development, the confusion is magnified to the point of despair.

Be thinking here of the confusion that some young people must sort out: the taunting of them by the papal bullies ("Homosexuality is a grave, grave sin."), the fear of rejection by family if the young person wants to "come out" as gay or lesbian, employment problems, and so on. Christ Almighty, it's a wonder that anyone is sane or achieves any happiness.

CHAPTER 10: FLAGELLATIO AND CRAS CATENELLAE

The moment we Novices of the class of 1952 set foot at St. Francis Xavier Novitiate, the word "Long Retreat" struck fear into our hearts. The Long Retreat was called the Spiritual Exercises of Ignatius Loyola. These exercises were thirty days of silence (no periods of recreation), prayer, penance, meditation, and reflection. Father Master conducted it. Everyone said it would transform a guy.

In my case I think that it did, in the sense that I felt like I had achieved something. As a result of the Long Retreat, I believed that I could present myself to the Jesuit Order and take vows of poverty, obedience, and chastity.

Many years later, when I had lost all belief in both the Church and the Order, my opinion about the Long Retreat has not changed. I was glad I had this experience, even though I'll not be going back for a second dose.

The Spiritual Exercises were divided into four weeks. The first week consisted of meditations on these Last Things: The Providence of God, Death, Hell, Punishment, and a desire to lead a godly life.

During the first week, it was expected that you make a general confession of all your sins and wayward deeds. For me, this served to separate me from my entire previous life. In fact I had no sins to confess. All I had to carry to my general confession were many gallons of stray spermatozoa deposited on various mattresses in the Great Pacific Northwest. Also, I had quit beating off when I first applied to the Jesuits when I had graduated from high school.

Even so, when, during the first week, I knocked on Father Master's door and entered, I had a grim feeling that I was at a pivotal point in my life. It was the act of general confession itself that was the task at hand, not any load of sins I carried around.

In the Jesuits, when you go to confession, there is no doleful curtain between you and the priest.

Father Master sat facing the window of his room. You, the wretched sinner, knelt by his side, hands folded, facing the same direction.

Obviously, Father Master knew who you were. The entire setting made it difficult to bullshit him. And so, I didn't even try. This is good. Bullshitting other folk was not one of my sins. Bullshitting myself, however, was another question.

Even so, the general confession was a struggle for me, though I had nothing real to confess. Remarkable rationalization. The general confession made you think that your entire life was on the line, do it right, once and for all, and you belong to Loyola for keeps. You're in! No more confusion about what you are doing with your life. Ah, ha! Security and wholeness in one fell swoop.

The Long Retreat begins. The first day's meditations (there were four meditations a day, forty-five minutes each) are about how God has brought the world into his plans. I'm feeling it right away. I want to be part of this. And, of course, I am, since I'm Irish and really good-looking!

The next day, however, the meditations on death begin. You are to imagine lying in your coffin, your flesh rotting and stinking. The casket is being lowered into the dirt.

You, Wretch, are gonna die, and are all but dead even now. Acknowledge your unworthiness, and confess that only God the Merciful can forgive your sins. The flames of hell are licking around your limbs. This is how you will wind up, Brother Casey. Don't try to get out of it, coward.

Each one of us dies, but the Jesuits are gonna capitalize on it. You die, and the Jesuits get your soul.

The effect on me was that I became convinced that I had to do something with my life, so worthless was I. I was not actually emotional, but certainly anxious about my soul. (I could be going to hell, perhaps marked out by some disease or other, perhaps syphilis even. I would be known as a reject from the Jesuit Order; or so I imagined.)

Sensory deprivation has its effects on me: silence, silence, and absolutely no talking to anyone.

The third or fourth day of the first week is about the Final Judgment. You stand before God. He looks at you. He is all-knowing. You can't hide. And what will I have to say in my defense? Can I say that I didn't fool around with the young girls at the Hillyard swimming pool? Is that enough to get me by? Nah! Dig deeper, Casey. Did I lie? Cheat? Steal? Are there marks of sin and muck on my soul? Will I be able to look God in the face, and say I have tried to live right, and be helpful to my fellows walking the same path? Will I be able to say, Look, Lord, behold: I do not have syphilis?

At this point I made my general confession, which I have told you about.

But now I must speak to you about Abnegation of the flesh. The flesh in question is your body. With the Jesuits, you beat your flesh, but not your meat.

We all had been told about this before the Long Retreat began, but I, for one, certainly did not grasp its significance. The first episode began about the second day of the Long Retreat, with the Death and Hell meditations.

Beating the flesh was in the form of the Flagellatio (Latin for "whip"). Do not confuse Flagellatio with Fellatio. We all called it the "Flahge" (rhymes with "garage").

The whip was a tightly knotted cord. It had a handle, and three lash-like cords parted out from the handle. The whip was about two feet long. Nasty knots ran the length of these cords. Each novice was given this instrument of torture. It was expected to last your entire life. (Imagine some Jesuit wearing his out!)

Here is the drill: supper in silence from six to six forty-five. Then kitchen chores to seven-thirty. Then you walk (still in silence, always silence) to the Novice end of the building. Then it's mincing steps to the Novice bulletin board. Only one bulletin is posted there: A small card, handed down from Ignatius himself, is pinned to it. The card is printed, "Hac Nocte Flagellatio." (Tonight, the whip.)

You know what it means. You were handed your flahge several weeks previously. But the insult is so cruel, that you consider walking down the hill and hitchhiking to Spokane. Instead, you stifle your tears and suck your thumb.

Now you have from seven-thirty p.m. to nine p.m. to think about the hac nocte Flagellatio. There is spiritual reading from a soporific book about Jesuit Martyrs, some brief prayers out of a small black book. Then you go to the chapel with the entire community for the mind-numbing litanies.

Then it is, quick! now back to your cubicle.

This is a communal exercise, but you don't see your fellow novices because the room beadle has turned out the lights.

Twelve guys in a room, each stripped to the waist, stand at attention, flahge in hand, waiting for the bell to ring.

What bell?

The bell of doom that the chief beadle rings. The first ring sounds at nine-o-five. It is the get-ready-to-abnegate-the-flesh bell. About two minutes later – and two minutes is a long time for you, naked to the waist, whip in hand, to meditate on the sins of the flesh (been thinking about Bridget Bardot, were you?).

Then it's ring number two, and you and your mates start the lashing. Criss-cross, the flahge goes on your back.

Father Master had instructed us that the Flagellatio is merely nominal. It's not how hard you swing the flahge, but the spirit of mortification of the flesh that counts. He didn't want anyone to overdo it lest the local sheriff came to investigate a novice's death from an accidental overdose of Flagellatio.

Recall that Jesus Christ Himself was tied up and whipped by Pontius Pilate and some Tea Party Activists. You see this in all the great paintings of the Renaissance. Does Michael Casey, a sensible Irish lad, want to follow in the footsteps of his master, Jesus Christ Himself? Sure he does. Admit it, it's all there in your vocation to Loyola's Militia. So, swing that flahge and follow in the footsteps of Christ.

Thus, you go along with this insanity because once you enter the Novitiate, you become a dum-dum for Loyola and give up your free will.

You swing the flahge and then you believe. Action precedes belief.

The purpose of this nasty ritual is to humiliate you. These two go together: you swing and you are humiliated. Humiliated by yourself! If you don't do it, who will?

Indeed this is sick stuff. You're thinking, maybe this would be O.K. for some Shiites in Iran, but all of us are Americans, normal guys. Yet normal guys must be transformed into imbeciles for the Kingdom of Christ.

We did this. We really did. But don't think you can understand this because you just can't. But we did it. We really did.

An irrational surd lies at the heart of all religious teaching. I don't mean simply "illogical". I mean irrational, that which cannot be penetrated by human comprehension. Once, it occurred to me, "Well don't swing so hard during the next session of flagellation." Indeed, once I took it easy, just tap, tap. Afterwards I felt guilty for fudging. I disliked myself for swinging so easy. Can you see the force of mind control in all of this?

The supreme triumph of the Grand Inquisitor is to produce an agent who transforms his own agency into servility. Allen Dulles, Richard Helms, and others, had to use drugs and sensory isolation to make their minions into M-K Ultra zombies. But Loyola did it with notice on the bulletin board, and a small white cord.

It takes mindless guts to swing the flahge, but it takes much more guts to say, "This is bullshit." But I didn't have the courage or experience to say this until many years later, and much humiliation had passed.

After the flagellation, you put on our shirt and throw a towel over your shoulders, grabbed your toothbrush and go to the balneum (toilet and sink area). This was a couple of urinals, a few toilets, a couple of showers, and a long stainless steel trough about twelve feet long. About eight faucets stuck out over this stainless steel gutter. You brushed your teeth and watched used toothpaste and choice goobers flow past to the center drain from upstream. Just the visual aid to cap off the hac nocte Flagellatio. All this is in silence: Magnum Silentia, Grand Silence.

There could be no eye contact with your fellow novices. There were no words spoken with the hoplites of the Lord, such as, "How did the flagellatio work out for you, Herb? Mine was really penitential. St. Ignatius would be really proud of me. Boy, oh, boy!" In fact, any eye contact was strictly verboten, at all times except during recreation. After brushing your teeth, you went to bed on your two inch thick mattress, purchased from the US Army Surplus right after World War I.

It's now nine forty-five, and you crawl into the sack and sleep like a log until five a.m.

But that flahge, God! how I came to dread it.

Once upon a time, the renowned Czech author, Franz Kafka, paid a visit to the novitiate. He was on a book tour for his novel, The Trial, whose main protagonist and victim was Michael K.

He read parts of this great philosophical novel to us, and then there were questions.

The first question was from Gordon Moreland, who knew all things. He asked "just how a Jew like Kafka had the gumption to preach to us, God's chosen?"

Kafka looked us all over, and said, "Say, is that Michael C sitting next to you." I squirmed in confusion and bewilderment. I squealed, "How did you know my name?" This could be dangerous to me, I thought.

Kafka said, "Michael K, Michael C-- you can tell the difference, huh?"

Well, he had me. His novel, The Trial, is of universal significance. Then he added, "You should be honored that your name is used to represent "universal insanity."

I didn't know what to say, so confused was I. Especially, since I had never read one of his books. At that time, very few folk in America had.

Kafka continued. "I would like to read to you an episode that I omitted from the original The Trial." I told him, "Go for it, Franz."

I can't remember all of what Franz Kafka read to us, but the gist of it is this:

Michael C is accused of a nameless crime. Of course, he doesn't know what the crime is. Neither, apparently, do the judges and magistrates at the trial.

You say, "What the fuck?"

Nevertheless, these guys are gonna kick ass. By God, they are.

At this outcry, the magistrates tell the orderlies to beat Michael C, or Michael K, whichever. The orderlies beat Michael K or Michael C. They have truncheons and small but nasty white whips. These whips were made by hand by some cloistered nuns in eastern Poland. They continue beating for some minutes. The beaters are big guys, linebackers with big muscles. Then, they switch to chains to really get the point across. Even so, Michael C does not get the point, nor does he know or recall how he got into this mess. Sometimes, he screams, "What is your fucking point?"

The beaters do not answer. They wear hoods over sunglasses.

This goes on, and eventually, the orderlies get tired. They call in reserves. One looks much like George St. Hilaire. In time, even these guys get tired. Then they say, "Well, shithead, you beat yourself.

We're going on our lunch break; we are having ravioli, red snapper, and red wine from Tuscany."

I plead, "What about me?"

Their Kaput says, "Always thinking of yourself, aren't you? Well, get over it. When we come back from lunch, we have more ideas in store."

I scream out, "I want lunch too!"

The Kaput says, "For you, a dog turd sandwich. But it's on rye."

So, Michael C began to beat himself. And kept at it for many years.

The flagellation is to produce a lashing on you. The better to make you Christ-like, who himself was lashed. "What?" you say. You don't get the connection? Well, neither did I nor other lash-ees. Recall, dear reader, the irrational surd that I spoke of.

After the long retreat, a few naïve souls wrote letters home to mom and dad. These were intercepted by Father Master. These lads got a lecture, during which the letter was ripped to pieces. Father Master said to the lads, "Just keep all this to yourselves. Tell no one. You are Jesuits-to-be, and must carry these secrets to the grave."

The other part of abnegation of the flesh was conveyed to us by another card on the bulletin board: "Cras Catenellae," "Tomorrow the chains."

Christ Almighty! Does this shit ever end?

What are the chains?

Think of large staples – the kind that electricians use – with pointed sharp ends, U-shaped, and woven together with long wire fasteners to form a belt or arm band. You were handed two such specimens, one for your leg and one for your arm. The design was meant to stick into your flesh but not pierce it. Father Master, ever moderate himself, said, "If blood flows, you've gone too far."

I told you he was an Aristotelian, "nothing to excess." I both praise and hate Aristotle. He is the philosopher who O.K.'d the use of chains, provided you don't bleed. Punishment in moderation.

The sharp points were to grip your flesh, just enough that the chains would not fall off. You leapt out of bed at 5 a.m. when a loud buzzer bell rang in the hallway. This buzzer alone was enough to sterilize the unwary.

The arm chain first: around your biceps it went, its staple-like points dug into your manhood. (Remember, it had to be tight enough not to fall off as you walked to the communion rail.) If it fell off, you were outed as a laggard and not a true soldier of Christ. You might even be asked to leave the Order, branded as a coward.

"Casey was kicked out of the Jesuits because his leg chain fell off while taking communion."

But the real pisser was the chain around the thigh. On it went, real tight. You walk down the steps (three flights) to the first visit in the chapel from 5 a.m. to 5:30, then back up the three flights. The genuflection was the worst. You bend your knee and hope you don't break into tears. A nasty humiliation that you can never talk about. Mother of Christ! Forgive me!

It's back to your cubicle for an hour of meditation on the life of Christ (maybe he's walking the Sea of Galilee with his leg chain strapped on his divine thigh). The meditation lasts one hour, from 5:30 to 6:30. And you're kneeling at your desk, the whole fucking time. Why? Why? Why? Because you're stupid, that's why. Your stupidity, born of inexperience and dishonesty, is the Church's Glory.

Now, here's the real gossip on the chains: some guys would lay the chains on the radiator next to their cubicle. Warm chains are not as sterilizing as cold ones, you dig? Then these guys would hook the leg and arm chains together, forming a belt, and strap it around their middle, like a belt. But with the points sticking out!! I am not making this up!

This was scandalous but guys did it. Me? Ho! Never, hah!

When I was in the novitiate, the word "double-think" was not in use. "Double-think" was a word invented to characterize those mental operations brought to light after, say, the Korean War. The popular term nowadays is "denial." This period of America history is most famous for the use of the term "brain-washing". These are not scientific terms, but quite telling nevertheless.

I say, it's possible for a guy to be submerged in double-think, and really approve of it, perhaps even liking it. The instrument of this process is the Spiritual Exercises of Ignatius Loyola.

Mike Casey, a foot soldier in Loyola's Army, stood in his trench atop a hill overlooking the Yamhill River and Sheridan, Oregon. He swung the whip and strapped on the chains. It was not as ghastly as what happened to American G.I.s in Korea, but it was real and involved the same double-think. Without double-think, the abnegation of the flesh simply could not work. Action precedes belief. You swing the "flahge" and you then believed that this imbecility pleased Christ Our Lord.

But what happens, in the years to come, when you stopped swinging or wearing the chains?

What does happen is that you are left with the VOID! Then, how are you going to fill the Void?

After four years at the Novitiate, I never used the whip or chains again. And I never heard anyone ever speak of it again. Even the crazies gave it up.

Thus the void grew and grew until some of us came to appreciate our humanity, at some cost, and just walked away from it all. But that was a decade or so away, and we all had to wait for Pope John XXIII to give us the key to the gates to our own lives.

There were still two weeks left in the Long Retreat. It is still silence per omnia secula seculorum ("forever and ever, world without end"). No letters from Mama or Papa, or Dominic, or Margaret.

When Eisenhower beat Stevenson to the White House, during the first week of November, 1952, Terry Corrigan, the most intelligent guy in our class, knew of it the next morning. He told me, and others, and soon it was all over the Novitiate.

Of course, Father Master was informed of this betrayal of silence (yes, who was the rat?). I think the rat's name rhymes with George St. Hot Air.

Father Master gave a very stern lecture about this. He was pissed! Your ass has not been blistered until Fr. Master scorched it, I'll tell you that. I pitied Terry Corrigan, who was by now shaping up as my best friend (but no talking).

The second week was actually ten full days. The first four days were on the "hidden life of Christ – his birth, his bar mitzvah, choosing the apostles, etc.

Next was a two-day stiff come-to-terms series of meditations on the TWO STANDARDS: the standard of Lucifer versus the standard of Christ. Under which standard will you take up your stand?

"Gee, Father Master, when you put it like that, I believe I'll go with the Standard of Christ."

A 'standard' is a military term. It was a tall pole with a banner waving from the top. Soldiers are meant to gather around it, regrouping or preparing to plunge into battle.

In these meditations, Father Master was at his most eloquent. His voice was firm and rhythmic, saying how reality was, this is your time to go full force into a life devoted to the Kingdom of Christ. He was not "preachy" or emotional. He was himself. I can still remember his plain example.

Of course, in time, I myself fell away from the Standard of Christ. But so had the entire Catholic Church and the Jesuit Order. I became merely flotsam and jetsam on the river of Vatican Two. But, back in 1952, I was persuaded by Father Master and the Long Retreat that the Standard of Christ was for me. And I wanted to be part of it.

I personally couldn't groove on the Satan or Lucifer stuff. But Father Master read to us from the New Testament about Lucifer swooping Christ up to the top of some high mountain. From there Lucifer showed Christ the riches and wealth of the entire world, and said, "They are all yours, Christ. You can have it all. See just over there, that's Madonna, Tom Cruise, and Lady Gaga frolicking and having a ball."

But Christ wasn't having any of it. He says to Lucifer, "No, Evil Sir! I shall go off into the desert and fast for forty days and forty nights. Maybe eat some thistles and snare some squirrels for my food.

Maybe hunt sea gulls with the Mormons. After all, the Mormons got rich off the desert." Many folk are not so sure that Lucifer and Christ had this conversation. But Michael Casey, Jesuit Novice in Training, lines up under the Standard of Christ.

After the first fifteen days of the Long Retreat, no mail from home, no news from the outside world, no whispering to your buddies at all, just silence, and it's on to the third week, the Passion and Crucifixion of Christ.

Next, it's on to the fourth week, the resurrection of Christ from the dead, I'm with it all the way, with my adolescent resolve still in place. The final meditation was called The Contemplation for Obtaining Love. This was a sort of release valve from the grind of the previous twenty-nine days. Since I never understood this meditation, I won't try to explain it. You'll just have to enter the Cave of Silence and Mortification yourself and eat the thistles. Then you too can be a full zombie in the Army of Loyola.

There it is: thirty days of silence, peer group pressure, and you are ready for combat to advance the Kingdom of Christ.

CHAPTER 11: THE WALTZ OF THE BUTCHER KNIFE JESUITS

After the Long Retreat, the rest of the first year as a Novice was mostly grin and bear it. I felt O.K. I liked the daily order, the structured companionship, the food was actually very good, some sports like basketball and handball, some baseball (but no touch football because it was against the rule of Tactus (touch), and many long walks around the surrounding fields and countryside. In the summer there was much berry-picking. There was also much work on the farm, baling alfalfa and stacking it on an Army surplus truck to haul it to the silo. I always wanted to drive the truck, but the guy in charge, the Kaput of the alfalfa brigade, pushed me aside and took the job for himself. This was training for the vow of obedience, actually the most odious of the three vows.

By the end of the first year I was well numbed out, and knew there was no exit for me. So, I stayed for the second year.

The second year, at the end of which you were "allowed" to take the three vows of Poverty, Chastity, and Obedience, was much like the first year.

But in my case there was one significant near-disaster.

The near-disaster scene occurred in the kitchen while the main meal was in progress. The meal was called "first table" and there was reading during it. Some novices are waiting on tables while a few other novices are in the kitchen area scrubbing pots and pans. The waiters and the scrubbers will eat later, during "second table."

While the main meal is in progress, the scrubbers must be very quiet so that the reading for that day can be heard by the assembled brethren.

At the end of the main meal, Father Rector, the head of the entire community (not Father Master), says "satis" (Latin for "enough"). Then the reader begins to read the Roman Martyrology for that day.

The scrubbers cannot be talking and must keep the noise down in the kitchen as the reader intones that "on this the third day of July,

433 A.D., St. Gertrude of Ravenna has her breasts cut off by Roman Legions and then she died."

Great, just great, what a way to end a good meal. And silence must prevail even into the pot scrubbing area in the kitchen.

Sometimes, silence does not prevail, or maybe Father Rector is sulking. Whatever. Sometimes Father Rector yells out, "Hey, too much noise. Everybody, please be quiet, for garsh sake." This man, in a snit, has been known to leap from his dining chair, rush into the kitchen to ream some ass on those noisy novices scrubbing pots in silence.

Father Rector blasts everyone in the kitchen. "We can't hear about Saint Gertrude of Ravenna getting her breasts cut off. Why can't you show some respect for the Rule of Silence, or for your brothers in Christ who really want to hear about Saint Gertrude getting her breasts cut off. What's wrong with you? Have you no respect? Don't make so much noise!"

Now, let me return to my near significant disaster. The cook on that day was Brother Ryan, S.J. He was a decent cook but an utter lunatic. In Jesuit jargon, Brother Ryan was a lay brother with vows, an actual member of the Jesuit Order, but not studying for the priesthood.

Brother Ryan was crazy. Just stark schizoid, psychotic, the original lone-nutter. When he ran the kitchen, a novice had to perfectly obey his orders or his commands. There could be no back talk. Again, this was more training for the vow of obedience. Ryan was not a Novice, and therefore his superior was not Father Master but Father Rector, whose name was Father Joe Logan, S.J. He was in charge of the entire Novitiate.

Father Rector would allow Brother Ryan only very dull and well-used razor blades since he had several times tried to slash his throat. And then there were his cheeks sunken from fasting.

But his eyes! Christ! They were not even the proverbial piss-holes in the snow banks. They were like crushed and bleeding roadkill.

Once a week, it was Brother Ryan who cooked the main meal. During it, he stayed in the kitchen fiddling with the stove. Next to the stove were two large tubs, one for scrubbing the big pans and the other filled with scalding hot water for rinsing the stainless steel serving pans.

Rudy Weinhandle was in the first tub, Mike Casey at the second tub, daring to stick his bare hands into the scalding water to deftly pull the steel pan out, and place it on the stainless steel countertop to dry off. The main meal was still in progress, and since there was reading from some pious book during the meal, you had to be very quiet, otherwise Father Rector would come charging into the kitchen and bawl you out. But when Mike Casey sticks his mortal hand into the scalding water and yanks out the steel pan, does he gently set it down on the stainless steel counter? Yeah, sure. He gives it a flip and it clatters like Lucifer's cymbals at the gates of hell.

After a bit Brother Ryan comes to me from behind and says, "No more noise." I say, "Yes, Brother Ryan, I'll be quiet." I mean this. But the pans are hot, and my mitts are tender already. A couple more times and I set the pan down easy. By now my mitts are killing me and I want to scream with pain. Then it's back to the loud clatter while my back is to Brother Ryan.

Suddenly he spins me around and holds a large butcher knife near to my throat.

Sheer reflex kicks in, and I grab his forearm and just barely force it back a few inches. He's saying, "I said no more noise."

When he spoke, the spell he was in seemed to abate somewhat, and I got both my hands on his forearm and pushed back as hard as I could but the fucker would not drop the knife. In all of this I had not said a word. Maybe a minute we stood there. The waltz of the butcher knife Jesuits.

Just then a waiter came into the kitchen for refills. The waiter saw us and said, "Whaa!" and then, "What's going on?" A knife at my throat, and he wants to gather information. That's Jesuit training for you.

Finally Ryan drops the knife to the floor, and I stomp on it with both feet. I let go of his arm and he returns to the stove. The waiter picks up the knife and puts it in the dirty knife bin.

Looney is one thing, but looney with a butcher knife is another. I stand and try to collect my wits. Then, at last, I return to the scalding water, the stainless steel pans and counter. But I'm looking over my shoulder all of the time.

All this makes for great novitiate conversation among the waiters and the rest of the kitchen help. By the end of the afternoon, the entire place knows of it. The word "knife" is mentioned and also the name "Casey."

In time even Father Rector knows of it, and he tells Father Master of the matter. The next day Father Master calls me into his office. He is sitting down at his desk but he does not tell me to sit. He says, "Brother Casey, I hear that you and Brother Ryan had an altercation. Is that so?"

"Altercation? Altercation? The crazy loon tried to kill me." I'm breathing heavy. I have survived a near-O.J. Simpson ordeal, and he calls it an altercation.

Father Master gets excited and starts to puff a bit himself. "No, he didn't try to kill you. Don't be crazy!" His voice is rising.

I blurt out, "He tried to kill me, he did, you weren't there."

"No, no, he didn't try to kill you. No he didn't. Don't be crazy!"

I buttoned my lip. If I said any more, he might send me back to Spokane. I had been in the Novitiate for nearly two years, and I wanted to stay.

Father Master dismissed me from his office, and I walked back to my cubicle. I had to think about this. And as you can tell, I'm still thinking.

Ah yes, the waltz of the butcher knife Jesuits, two Black Irish guys, Ryan and Casey, both of us from the bottom of the shit heap.

Since you no doubt are judicial rationalists, you want to know who was at fault, Ryan or Casey? He had the knife, but I was supposed to make no noise.

But, really, you want to know who was at fault, don't you? Yeah, maybe it was just a fuck-up. Even so, Mike Casey must pay the price. Ryan was nuts. Thus there is no price for him to pay since he has nothing wherewith to pay.

Obviously, Casey must pay since he is the innocent victim. He pays with his innocence and intellect. All payments will be processed through Father Master and Father Rector.

Whatever they decide, it is all fallacy, the fallacy of arm-chair ignorance.

My two-thousand dollar scholarship, my father's legacy to me, will not and does not impress them. I am nothing to them, just one-half of a fuck-up.

The decree that Casey was the guilty party ("don't make so much noise, garsh. Be quiet!") is founded on the need for Loyola's capos to produce tranquility and smooth order behind the cloistered curtain of the Peace of Christ.

Ryan had nothing to lose. He knew he was nuts and looney. He will not improve and he knows this. Casey has everything to lose, besides his Irish throat. Therefore Casey must pay, and keep his mouth shut, or at least not appeal to any higher authority (yeah, sure!).

The Jesuits do not have rights. They have a vow of obedience, Loyola's glue that holds the Kingdom of Christ together.

Your Honor, may I ask a what-if question?

"Permission granted."

"What if Ryan had slit my throat, and I bled to death at St. Francis Xavier Novitiate overlooking the Yamhill River. Yeah, what-if?"

What would the Jesuit capos do?

Would they have telephoned the local sheriff in Sheridan?

"Hey, Sheriff Dale, this is Joe Logan. We have a homicide up here at the Novitiate. Quick, you must investigate us all," says the worried Father Joe Logan.

Sheriff Dale Jones would no doubt say, "Investigate? Golly, Joe, I'm gonna let you handle your own internal affairs. I've got my hands full down here at the bottom of the hill. Besides, you guys don't pay property tax on your three thousand plus acres. We can't cover you. Sorry, Father Joe."

Joe Logan, God's busy bully, thinks to himself, "Thank God for Sheriff Dale Jones. I'm off the hook thanks to that property tax exemption. Glory be to God."

However, Father Joe would need some story to tell.

He convenes all members of the Jesuit community, about two hundred guys and twenty priests, into the chapel. Joe leads the rosary, and the dismal litanies. After the prayers, Father Joe stands before the assembled community. He wears a white starched linen chasuble and a purple stole around his neck. Also, he is full of himself, like George Steinbrenner before a Yankee World Series.

He announces: "Our Brother in Christ, Michael Casey, N. S.J. has passed away from a blood disorder from his throat. May he rest in peace."

The top Jesuits have a vow of obedience, and the professed fathers (the very top) have a special vow of obedience to the Holy Father in Rome. The Pope in question was Pope Pius the XII.

This is the pope who had revised and rewritten the Church's Canon Law. Its first canon states: "...Christ's sole vicar on earth is the bishop of Rome, the Holy Father. All authority comes from God, and the bishop of Rome is the sole authority on earth. What is bound by us on earth is bound in heaven."

With this in mind, it is clear to Father Joe Logan, S.J. that there is no need whatsoever, to call Sheriff Dale Jones to investigate Michael Casey's blood disorder at the St. Francis Xavier Novitiate at the top of the three thousand or so acres, all tax-exempt, overlooking the tranquil Yamhill Valley.

Was I a coward for not pushing back against Father Master when he told me that what I thought was black was actually white?

No, I was not a coward. I was a Jesuit. There is a famous principle in Loyola's Spiritual Exercises. It is: "The Jesuit must be ready, if the Church declares that what he sees as black is white, to agree with her, even though his senses tell him the opposite." When I entered the Jesuits, I had given up my free will, and I was prepared to do whatever I was told. I was young and had natural resilience. And so I swallowed the episode and the fright about the waltz of the butcher knife Jesuits.

What really stung, however, was Father Master's words that I was crazy, and that Ryan was not going to kill me.

146

Me, crazy, Ryan,...well, who knows?

The kitchen knife up to my throat. (And just what was it doing there?) If Ryan had drawn blood, it would be me sent back hitchhiking to Spokane with the stitches in my throat, not the lunatic Ryan.

What the Jesuits fear most is scandal. They are clumsy at cover-up. When they are exposed, as in their current pedophile mess, which has forced the Oregon Province into bankruptcy, they wring their hands and say, "Well, golly, we didn't know. Give us a break. We're not responsible. That goddamn Mike Casey shouldn't have made so much noise in the kitchen. Actually, it's his fault."

"Huh? What?" you ask. "Who? Brother Ryan? Never heard of him."

Indeed Black is White. Shut up now!

A few months later, I knelt along with about twenty other classmates at the foot of the altar of the Novitiate, and pronounced the three vows of Poverty, Chastity, and Obedience.

I thus passed into the next two years of the designated time of the Novitiate. These last two years were called the Juniorate, the study of Latin (a really big deal), Greek, English literature, History, and Rhetoric. These were called the Classics. Our superior was the aforementioned Father Joe Logan, S.J., the Father Rector, or as I, and a few others referred to him, Joe, the Busy Bully.

Besides these humanities studies, Joe would ensure that there would be yet more punishments and humiliations. His job as the Father Rector was to ensure that black is white.

CHAPTER 12: KNIVES AND THE BLOOD OF THE MICKEY

August 1954, now I am a Jesuit, a member of an esteemed religious order. Wow! I made it, didn't I?

In the Catholic Church's code of Canon Law, the term "religious" has a specified meaning. There, in that code, "religious" means "binding". The binding is just the three vows of poverty, chastity, and obedience. In today's popular parlance, "religious" means, we may suppose, an attitude or a feeling about heavy-duty questions, like abortion or creationism. Republican candidates for Congress are always "religious," i.e., reverential and pious. Mitt Romney was said to be "religious," and didn't he look and sound like it?

But in Canon Law, "religious" means binding. A member of a religious order is bound by vows. The word itself comes from a Latin word "religere", to bind by cords. Thus, Roman prisoners were "bound" by cords, as they were led to their execution by disembowelment.

In books about Ancient Rome, I have seen representations of victims, hands and feet bound. The forlorn wretch is strapped to an altar of stone, just like the lad Isaac in the Old Testament with his dad Abraham holding the knife, poised, like a sick fuck, for the sacrifice. In the representations a priest stands before the victim holding a large knife. The priest is about to slit the victim's throat. Sometimes the victim is a goat, a bull, or a sheep. It doesn't matter if the victim is human or just mammal. It's the blood gushing from the wretch's throat that placates the god.

This is the original source of the meaning of "religious." Jews do not have religious orders, nor do Protestants. The Anglicans have a few nuns (female religious) but the Brits are peculiar, are they not? Actually it's the blood gushing out of the wretch's throat that convinces you that this is real stuff. God is appeased by blood, the blood of the victim.

Have I not here summarized the entire teaching of the Church about Christ's Atonement?

Behold, The Lamb of God. This brings me to the social hierarchy in the slitting of the victim's throat. At the bottom level is the Jewish peasant who can afford a small lamb. This lamb's blood will wash away any lapses in the peasant's observance of the Law.

The peasant brings the lamb from his pasture to the Temple. He gives the priest five dollars. The priest, with suitable mumbo jumbo, slashes the lamb's throat, then splashes the blood on the peasant so that all can see he is now kosher. Washed in the blood of the lamb.

Let us now ascend the social ladder to some city even wealthier than Jerusalem, say, Cairo or Alexandria. These folk have real money for the blood ritual. A bull, for example, is certainly more impressive than a lamb. When his throat is slashed, it's like huge bombs going off.

A very important man, say, the amazing George Sore Ass, needs validation (and perhaps a tax deduction). George purchases a large bull, perhaps the famous Taurus of astrological fame.

For the bull, a special altar is built. The bull is on a platform raised about four feet above the temple floor. Holes are drilled in the platform, and the bull is tied down by strong cords. The bull bellows and snorts. "This is not fair at all," he bellows. "What have I done to you, to deserve this?" The bull knows what's coming.

The purchaser, and maybe his family, crawl under the platform. The important man and his entire family all wear ceremonial garments, maybe even magical underwear. This is a blood ceremony, after all. The priest approaches the bull, his ceremonial knife in hand. The bull cannot defend himself. But he bellows with all his might.

"Poor Mr. Bull. Your time is up. But you will serve a higher cause," says the priest. The priest then slits the bull's throat. The blood gushes forth and streams down through the floor of the platform, and down onto George Sore Ass and his family. He has paid for this. And he wants all to know of this. Especially since bulls cost a lot of money. George and his family are washed with real blood. At last they are saved. Everyone who knows this family thinks highly of him, and pay him honor and tribute.

The next day, George scans the local paper for a write-up about the sacrifice. For the sacrifice to be valid, it must be seen to be bloody, hence the notice in the paper.

The bull's blood makes a big splash, and word of this wonderful event reaches to some wealthy citizens of Rome. They have a confab, and decide that they can do better. After all, Rome is the center of the Empire. Their spokesman, Pio Nono, the Pius Pope of the Pius People, has a large budget. Scouts are sent forth to the outer reaches of the Empire to solicit an actual human being (males preferred).

At first a club-foot with a hare-lip is sent from Albania. Pius is insulted. "Albanians are not Catholic, they are not Baptized. Besides I want a perfect specimen. And don't pawn off on me any Italian boys, you know, the castrati. That would look cheap."

The scouts journey to Ireland. They find a gorgeous Mickey near Sligo, good feet, no hare-lip, blue eyes, blond hair. The scouts ship him to Rome. Pio Nono says, "Perfect, I'll take him. How much?"

The pope constructs his own papal platform, much higher than the one for the bull. On the appointed day the Pope and his entourage assemble under the platform. Then the priest, his stipend in hand for his services, approaches the Mickey, now bound hand and foot. He asks him if he wants absolution from his sins.

The Mickey, knowing his fate, screams, "What sins? You fucker! Your sins, not mine."

The priest then slits the Mickey's throat, and the blood gushes and flows down through the floor onto Pio Nono and his pals.

On that day Ireland became a Catholic country, with its own Cardinals and Archbishops and Bishops and Monsignors and pedophiles galore, O! Jesus, you don't know the half of it. Forgive me my digression about the Irish and the sacrifices of the victims, who are now known in Canon Law as religious.

CHAPTER 13: BLACK IS WHITE

After first vows, the entire class of 1952 moved to the Juniorate section of St. Francis Xavier Novitiate. Our new superior was Father Joe Logan, S.J. His title was "Father Rector". I always called him (under my breath) "Joe the Busy Bully."

Joe was a big guy, had been a terrific athlete, and still was. He had a huge chest and a full head of hair on top of an Irish monkey-faced head. He communicated with you by walking fast up to you, full chest maneuver, and just dumping his importance all over you.

Here's how I remember the bestial Joe: Suppose you were a dog and were invited to go camping with Mitt Romney, you know, on top of the Romney car. Well, that's the relationship of me to Joe the Busy Bully.

At last I was a Junior, that is, I studied Latin, Greek, English, and History. These were called the classics.

When the subject comes up, I can say to people, "I majored in the classics." This impresses people. And it's very elitist.

The entire group of us were divided into two groups: the "A" class and "B" class. This applied only to Latin and Greek. I was in the "A" class. But I was uncomfortable with this elitist baloney in Loyola's Army. And after a semester, I was demoted to the "B" class. This was the decision of Joe the Busy Bully. But I was O.K. with it since I didn't like the pressure in the "A" class where my classmates were very fluent in Latin and Greek, while I was just so-so there.

What I didn't understand at the time was that all of us were being sorted out: just who would be the future Jesuit leaders and big cheezes, and just who would be the grunts in the trenches. And it's looking, isn't it, that Mike Casey is headed to grunt-dom.

At the time, if you were a stand-out in Latin and Greek you were headed to the star category of Jesuit status. At least in the Oregon Province, the hysteria then was Latin, Latin, and only Latin. Ha, I love this: nowadays the Jesuits don't even bother with Latin. That was then, brother, this is now. Now Jesuits are hip, and delivering the Loyola doctrine to the modern world where no one gives a shit about fluency in Latin. All that matters now is how much money

156

a Jesuit can shake down from some pathetic philanthropist. Me? I'm not a philanthropist; I'm just pissed.

But the Latin class was the really big deal. Every day we were given an exhortation as to the crucial importance of Latin since all of the Church's Philosophy (Aquinas) and Theology (more Aquinas) were in Latin.

May I point out to you that in the seven years I studied philosophy and theology, not one class was ever taught in Latin.

But the exams, all of them oral, were in Latin. Go figure. Not one class was taught in Latin! Ever!

All of us were glad of this. But all of us wondered as to who or what was running the Jesuit Order. And what is going on here? Latin hysteria and then no Latin classes in philosophy or theology?

Back to the Juniorate in 1954: We grunts in the "B" class were assigned under the tutelage of Father Conny Mullin, a short but very stout baseball pitcher from San Francisco. He pitched there before World War I. He reminded us of this fact quite often. He also occasionally mentioned the San Francisco earthquake. He was maybe sixty-five or seventy years old. And he had mastered Bradley's Arnold.

The latter was a Latin grammar exercise book originally written by Matthew Arnold, of Victorian literature fame, and updated by someone named Bradley.

The exercises were dense and quite difficult to comprehend. Pure abstract Latin for the Glory of God. Never once was there any meaning or context to these exercises. On one page would be a list of ten sentences, complex and compound, which you had to translate into a precise Latin that even Cicero would appreciate. On the next page was another list of ten sentences in Ciceronian Latin. These you were to render into idiomatic English: Like Sisyphus pushing his rock to the top of the mountain, only to have it roll back down, just inches from the top. Bradley's Arnold and Sisyphus working together to make the world of the Jesuit grunts meaningful for a week or so.

You did your homework and handed in your exercise to Father Conny Mullin, S.J. He would talk about that day's exercise. Then he would hand back the previous day's exercises, all marked up in red ink.

Here's the deal: you were to make note of these corrections, attending to the appropriate Ciceronian nuances, and then hand them back to Father Conny Mullin, S.J. These exercises he did not hand back to us. In fact he kept them, each and every one of them; he stored them in his file cabinet in his room. Thus, he, and he alone would have a master copy of Bradley's Arnold. Virtual proprietary information for Father Conny.

Father Conny feared that these exercises could be handed down to next year's class, if he did not secure every one of them. And he did secure them, by God, he did. No one would throw a curve ball past Conny, the Jesuit baseball pitcher. He had nothing else to do, besides hover like a hawk over Bradley's Arnold.

The exercises from Latin to English were to be translated into idiomatic English. For example, "Tempus coepit" was to be rendered as "He took time by the forelock." In this way Victorians would understand you if you ever suffered the misfortune of having to speak to the Victorian Matthew Arnold, or to Queen Elisabeth or her son Prince Charles the Putz. "Hello, there! Prince Putz, I hear you took time by the forelock. Is that so?" Is it any mystery that the British selected their code breakers from their top classical scholars?

One day, it came to pass that he handed back to me my exercise, and it had no red marks on it. I had actually translated this particular exercise perfectly. Could someone in the "B" class actually do this? But I had.

But there was no praise forthcoming to me from Father Mullin, the baseball pitcher who was a contemporary of Abner Doubleday and President William McKinley.

After class I returned to my cubicle and threw the perfect exercise into my wastebasket. Why save it? It was perfect. Thus I assumed I didn't have to hand it back in to Father Mullin.

After a few days Father Mullin calls me to his room, and asks, "Where's the exercise?" I tell him, "I don't have it." He says, "Whaah?" I say, "I threw it away."

Well, you would think I had thrown dirty dishwater in his face. He took my answer as a total insult, an affront to Bradley's Arnold.

He said, "I want that exercise back. Go find it."

I try again. "But I threw it away," I plead.

"No you didn't. Bring it back to me." In his mind, it is as though Mike Casey is saying that the San Francisco earthquake did not happen.

Back and forth this went until at last he dismissed me from his room.

The next day, Father Rector, Joe, the Busy Bully, calls me into his office. It's the same interrogation. He asks, "Where's the exercise?" He is sitting and I am standing.

I say, "I threw it away."

He says, "No, you didn't. You have to give it back to Father Mullin."

In these pages, brothers and sisters, I have mentioned several times how Franz Kafka read to us novices and juniors at St. Francis Xavier Novitiate selections from his novel The Trial wherein the anti-hero, Michael K or Michael C, whichever, hears his fate read out to him. He is accused of a crime; no one knows what the crime is, but it is definitely a crime; and be sure now that Michael will be convicted, regardless.

And, why? Because Black is White, goddammit, so just shut up.

The Inquisition of Joe, Conny, Mickey Casey, all Irish guys, goes on for several days.

Mullin does not yield nor does the Bully. The Bully lets me know that I have to solve this problem. There are no innocent foot soldiers in Loyola's Army. This is the message I got. If I want any peace of mind, I will have to create the perfect Bradley's Arnold exercise. "Go for it, kid," whispers the Holy Ghost into my ear. "Take time by the fucking forelock. Tell them what they wanna hear."

I listen to the Holy Ghost, and proceed to recreate the perfect Bradley's Arnold exercise.

Crushed, dazed, and humiliated, I do exactly that.

Black is White! So just fuck it, anyway.

The lesson about authority I thought I had learned from the Brother Ryan and the butcher knife episode, it seems, I must learn all over again.

And what is that lesson?

It is that these guys at the top of the Jesuit shitheap want not only obedience. They want to make you suffer. They need to humiliate you, to render you servile, to make you feel pain.

And most of the time it works. At least in the short run.

My last year at the Novitiate seemed to feel much different than the previous three years. I was still in the orbit of the Bully since he became the Latin teacher of the "B" class. And I worked hard at staying out of his line of fire.

On the positive side, our Greek teacher, Father Monahan, asked me if I wanted to be in his "A" class for Sophocles and Demosthenes. Monahan was a reactionary, but a cool one. Besides I liked his teaching style. It was analytic and Socratic. This meant that you could question and probe the text. In all, being "moved up" to his class meant that at least one teacher appreciated some ability in me.

The first semester was Sophocles' Antigone. I memorized in the original Greek the entire speech of Creon, the ruler of Athens. This speech is a masterpiece of rhetoric. The speech goes on for about ten minutes, and I delivered it to the class in my best rhythm and cadence. Monahan said I did a good job. After class, Terry Corrigan said it was terrific. It felt good that I got some validation from two people I respected. Maybe I was not the utter victim that you-know-who had made me out to be.

In the second semester, Monahan's course was Greek Rhetoric. This was mostly Demosthenes. Again I found my element. I made an idiomatic translation of one of his speeches. My written copy was about twenty-five pages long. I gave it to Monahan and he told me it was really well-done. Monahan had a very self-contained personality, and was not given to gushing praise on the lower ranks of the Lord's hoplites.

The entire second semester was devoted to Rhetoric. Allow me to recapture the original meaning of the word "rhetoric". It means the art of making a speech. This includes both composition and delivery. Nowadays it seems to mean a "sales pitch" or some gaseous whoop-de-do. But actually it means that there are rules based on logical reasoning. Thus, holy-rollers are disqualified.

Father John Dempsey was the speech teacher. He also was the corrector at table-reading. He was a stickler for pronunciation and phrasing. While reading, if you slumped into "becuz," he would say, "Correction, Brother. That word is "because." If you wanted to improve, he was the teacher for you. Most of the guys didn't particularly like him; he was a bit swishy, walked with a strut, and took pronunciation seriously. But he wasn't a prig, and I felt I could learn from him.

In the first year in the Juniorate, you composed and delivered a sermon in English. This was to be delivered at the evening meal. While my brothers in Christ were chewing on fried chicken, I was delivering my memorized sermon. My assigned topic was "Our

Mother Mary, Mediatrix of All Graces." Like a G.I. in Korea defending his bunker, I gave the sermon against the enemy of fried-chicken and noisy pots and pans.

As an orator I was just so-so. But I had guts. Which is what it takes to proclaim the wonders of the Blessed Virgin Mary to the assembled eaters of fried-chicken. Joe Logan chewed his chicken and stared at me.

The next year, each of us had to write, memorize, and deliver a sermon in Latin. This took place during Lent. It seemed a very fitting penance.

Once a week you wrote a speech or sermon and handed it in to Father Dempsey. Some of these he handed back with notations. You were also to visit his room every other week to go over your effort, and he would comment on it.

When I went there, I could see he liked me, and went to some effort to help me mature as a writer and a speaker. I got no bad vibes from him.

He had a small speech lab in the basement of the building. Before Dempsey introduced me to it, I had never heard of its existence. It had a tape recorder so you could actually hear what you sounded like. Remember, this was 1955-56, and such was not common equipment then. There was a full length mirror so you could practice your gestures. I took pleasure in what I heard and saw. Am I committing the sin of vanity? The only other mirrors in the Novitiate were small six by ten inch ones in the bathroom for shaving. Mirrors foster the vice of vanity. Their use was rationed since they were an occasion of sin.

By the Jesuit standards of the time Father Dempsey was the only teacher who was up to date. The rest were still at Bradley's Arnold stage, and still taking time by the forelock.

Father Dempsey took me into the lab. He analyzed my posture as I spoke, pointing out how I might improve. He also recorded me giving a soliloquy from Shakespeare and a speech from Edmund Burke which I had memorized. He indicated how I might improve my diction and articulation. All of this happened over a period of weeks. He and I were sequestered there in the small lab in the basement of St. Francis Xavier Novitiate. While the two of us were alone in the lab, I felt O.K., not exactly relaxed but not feeling like I'm alone in the bunkhouse in North Dakota with Bill Olson, the farm machinery salesman, on top of me humping away on my virginal belly.

In truth, my only apprehension was that other members of my class might know of Father Dempsey's attention to me and wonder what was going on in that room. In other words, that goddam Bill Olson was still on my back (or belly, if you are literal minded). I had never heard of Dempsey privately tutoring anyone else in the lab. It all seemed unusual.

None of this was funny-business or erotic. The guy was a teacher and thought he could open me up a bit as a human being, in line with my physical potential (i.e., my voice and appearance and posture). No one before this had ever noticed me in this regard. It gave me some hope and confidence that the Kafka Michael C had its limitations.

Father Dempsey was the main teacher in my four years at Sheridan, besides Monahan, that I truly appreciated. I learned from him. Probably, no one else did. But I did.

When the time came for the class of 1952 to finally leave the Novitiate I went to say goodbye to him in his room. It was the most positive personal experience for me of the whole four years. His face was beaming and he said what a pleasure it was to work with me. I knew he meant it. I had learned from him and had fashioned an ideal of what a teacher should be. This was very personal to me, there on that hill overlooking the Yamhill Valley. So what if he was a bit swishy and like good-looking Irish guys. Get over it, bro, not everyone is destined to be like the macho Joe-the-you-know-who.

CHAPTER 14: AQUINAS AND HAVELOCK ELLIS

Open any book about American history and you will find scant mention of the 1950's. Pages and pages of the 1960's, but the 1950's are mostly blank, like Eisenhower himself.

The entire class of 1952 was moved along (promoted?) to Mt. St. Michael's Philosophate. This was a large fortress style building built in 1919. It housed about two hundred Jesuits, scholastics, teachers, and some retired Jesuits.

Mount St. Michael's School of Philosophy was perched on a high hill overlooking the city of Spokane. At the very bottom of the hill was the aforementioned Hillyard swimming pool. Yes, I did often think of Jolene, and her adolescent girlfriends sunning themselves at the side of the pool. But that was then; this is now, and I am a vowed

Jesuit looking forward to reading Aquinas and Aristotle. This may be called regression to infancy.

The Jesuits had a system: it was Noviate, Philosophy, teaching high school (called regency), and Theology, followed by Ordination to the Priesthood. This took fifteen years to complete. The Jesuits called all of this formation. At the end of this marathon, the mind-numbed Mickey is so brain-dead that all he can think of is: when or how will he actually get laid.

The aforesaid Mickey pushes all of these questions down into his unconscious or scrotum, thus ensuring enriched confusion about the important forces of life.

Do not ask me why I endured this formation, sometimes even believing it. It is clear to me now, many years later, that the unconscious rules all. But that insight was no help to me back in the 1950's.

Thus, my class was there from 1956 to 1959.

I have told you how I gave up my free will when I joined the Jesuits. You didn't believe me when I said that. However, my career as a Jesuit student (scholastic) proves that I really was like Loyola's dead man (sicut cadaver). This is the core teaching of Loyola: take a living, breathing human Mickey and transform him into a cadaver.

At this time, the general of the Jesuits, Fr. John Baptistè Jansens, S.J., decreed that every Jesuit had to have a specialty. He had to have an assigned "major" besides the usual or "normal" course of study (i.e., Latin, Greek, Aquinas' philosophy, and, naturally, Aquinas' theology).

Some Jesuit bureaucrat, a savage prick named Fr. William Weller, S.J., visited with each of us during our last few months at Sheridan. He was the Province Dean of Studies. It was he who decided what you were to "major" in. He said to us to write down our first three choices for our "major". I wrote down: History, Mathematics, and Speech. Then the savage prick consulted with our superior, Joe the Busy Bully. Later when we all arrived at Mount St. Michael's, a notice was posted on the bulletin board with our names and assigned major. Mine was LATIN!

Joe the Busy Bully, just like Bill Olson, the buggering bastard in the bunkhouse in North Dakota, simply would not let go of me. Joe thought I would be a useful high school Latin teacher. So, fuck you, Joe.

All other members of the class were majoring in English (and thus reading real novels, like Hemingway) or History, or Economics, or Political Science, or Law (Terry Corrigan), or Mathematics, or Physics. But I must take a special course in Virgil's Bucolics from some Jesuit fruit (there were so many!). Why not just pour arsenic into my coffee?

The idea of each Jesuit having a specialty, according to our General Jansens, was so that Jesuit schools in the United States would be equal to, or on par with, the esteemed "secular" schools. All for the Greater Glory of God.

Weller was a prick, Logan was a bully and a prick. And Mike Casey was an orphan without a prick.

I was supposed to fortify my soul with prayer, fasting, and Latin. No "secular" enhancement for me while other classmates got degrees in Mathematics, Physics, or Law. Believe me, I'm not even slightly bitter.

The curriculum in philosophy was set by some high priest in Rome. He was called the Cardinal of the Sacred Penitentiary. I think he was the same guy who decreed the use of the cras catenallae and the flagellatio. At any rate, the entire philosophy curriculum came out of the writings of Thomas Aquinas.

Aquinas, a very fat man, had boiled down Aristotle's philosophy to one million pages of precise and very readable Latin. Aristotle himself never wrote any books. What is called The Works of Aristotle are actually the notes written down by his students.

But Aquinas made the best of it. I actually took pleasure in reading Aquinas, so clear and well-organized was his prose. The guy had an answer for everything. I nearly became a conservative just by reading his writings and listening to the lectures of my teachers. But I'm too Irish and working class to go all the way. In fact, as the school year progressed, Aquinas seemed to me to resemble Eisenhower; bland and Republican.

At the end of each year, an oral exam (not the kind a dentist gives, but even worse) lurked in the shadows. This exam was in Latin. The exam was composed of fifty theses (rhymes with feces). A thesis is a proposition whose truth was essential to the entire edifice of Catholicism. For example: The human soul is immortal.

During the exam, conducted by three Jesuit examiners, you were asked, in Latin, to defend one of the theses. The examiner chose which one. Each examiner got five minutes on you. Then it was on to the next examiner who would call out the number of some other thesis.

Then it was on to the next until your fifteen minutes of torture in Latin was up. In reality, the exam was a test of your ability to fake it in Latin. Thus, I passed. In the third year there, the exam lasted half an hour.

I had by 1957 been in the Jesuits for five years. I had received no encouragement from any teacher or superior, except from Fr. Dempsey, the speech and rhetoric teacher at Sheridan. Most of my Jesuit classmates were on the 'A' team while I was definitely on the 'B' team.

Was it me? Or was it the Jesuit system? I had no free will. Hence, it must be the Jesuit system. It was not for me to choose what to study. I went to the Latin seminar on Virgil's Bucolics, where I was the class dunce. Resentment and discouragement was my fate (in the 1950's no one spoke of 'depression', only of 'discouragement').

Unbeknownst to me, several wheels turned in the inner chamber of Who is Who? in the Oregon Province. Who? begins with Father Cliff Kossel, S.J. He was the Dean of the Philosophate. He taught the course in Ethics (the Natural Law). He also taught the course in Greek philosophy, Democritus through Plato. He was a serious guy but not a fanatic. The entire Oregon Province considered him its best philosopher.

In the course on Greek philosophy, I wrote my course paper on Plato's Symposium.

Kossel gave it an 'A minus'.

Terry Corrigan had volunteered to hand deliver the graded papers to all fifty members of the class. When Terry got to my room, he was shook with dismay. He told me that he (remember, he was the best read and most intelligent guy in our class) had received only a grade of 'C', and no one else had received even an 'A minus'.

The Jesuits did not publicly post individual grades (remember the sin of vanity?). Hence, no one of us actually knew whose star was on the up, and whose was headed into dunce city.

Each one of us received a B.A. degree from Gonzaga University just by enduring three years of Aquinas. Only Kossel decided who got an M.A. degree in philosophy. Owing to his influence and direction, and to the subsequent influence of Father John Leary, S.J., President of Gonzaga University (and a renowned pederast) I was eventually granted an M.A. degree in Philosophy from Gonzaga University. In this regard I was also coached by my classmate Don Davis, S.J. Later, had it not been for the M.A. degree I would have been without a meal ticket when I eventually left the Jesuits in 1969.

175

And, while I'm on the subject, both Kossel and Davis were from North Dakota. Every little bit helps.

As to my academic development, Kossel gave me a big break, via Terry Corrigan. Terry told me he spoke to Kossel about my Virgil's Bucolics situation. Kossel accordingly placed me in one of his seminars on Aristotle. I managed to fudge my way along in the Greek text. My perspective was that I was actually realizing some useful analytic skills. In fact, the text we were studying was Aristotle's Analytics.

It has always seemed to me that at certain turning points of my life, a key individual directed me into a better path or course of conduct. An example would be Terry Corrigan and Cliff Kossel. The Catholic Church and the Jesuits were no worse in the 1950's than they are now.

But back then some guys could make a difference for you as an individual. Nowadays this does not seem possible, especially since the Polish Pope joined the Catholic Church with the forces of darkness. The Pope and his buddies have so trivialized the life of the Spirit that I would be ashamed to attend Mass. There is just no Spirit in the Church. And if there is no Spirit, an individual can make no difference.

Apart from the regular curriculum and class lectures, I managed to rediscover my boyhood and adolescent interest in reading serious books. In grade school I read Tom Sawyer, Huckleberry Finn (which I read twice, so enchanting were Huck and Indian Joe), and Guadalcanal Diary, by Richard Tregaskis. In high school I read Big Sky, by Guthrie, and Across the Wide Missouri by DeVoto, and also The Oregon Trail by Parkman.

But at Mt. Saint Michael's, the library was open to all (except for one part, which I will later speak of). There I found Dostoyevsky and his novel, The Devils. My God, how that book thrilled me! Also, there was Kristen Lavransdatter, and Graham Green, and the novel titled, The Cypresses Believed in God, about the Spanish Civil War, and whose author's name I can't recall. But the book that really knocked me out was Leon Trotksy's The History of the Russian Revolution. This writing made me realize that very big events and causes were going on in the world far beyond what I was experiencing in the Jesuit Order. It did not make me want to leave the Order, but it gave me a far wider perspective on what I could believe. These books formed my judgment about what was valuable, as opposed to the ridiculous seminar on Virgil's Bucolics. I wanted a real education, not just a degree or some "major" courtesy of Fr. Weller or Joe Logan.

The part of the library that was not physically open was a small section in the rear of it. It was an alcove, about twenty feet long and about ten feet deep. Here's the deal: a heavy cyclone fence ran the length of this alcove. The fence rose from the floor to the ceiling. Two by fours formed the uprights for the cyclone fence. At one end of this was a gate framed by two by fours. The gate was also of cyclone fence construction. And on the gate was a massive padlock.

Inside the alcove were shelves of books which no Jesuit would ever get his mitts on. Only one Jesuit in the entire world had a key to the padlock. He was Fr. Tom McLaughlin, S.J., the librarian.

I often stood at the fence and peered at the books inside. It was not actually possible to read the titles, except for a few. One title I finally discerned had the author's name: it was Havlock Ellis. I looked his name up in the library's biographical dictionary.

Havlock Ellis' book was about sex!

I am not making any of this up.

But could a more potent symbol than a cyclone fence be used to warn us all that these were dangerous books? No one could read these books without incurring grave, grave sin. Let us praise the cyclone fence builders of the Lord for alerting us that evil abounded in certain books and not in the heart of the Cardinal of the Sacred Penitentiary. If I ever got my mitts on one of those books, in a flash I would lose my immortal soul. Just holding one of those books meant that I was in a state of sin, even before I read it. Maybe, if I wore certain sin proof gloves...Nah!...never mind the bother.

Seven years later when I returned to Mt. St. Michael's as a newly ordained priest, I visited the library. And the goddam cyclone fence was still there. The fence said that I should mend my free-thinking ways, or else. Certainly the cyclone fence demonstrated to anyone who could see what the Church really thought of any individual's mind or cognitive abilities.

During the years at Mt. Saint Michael's Philosophate I realized that I was a mere Jesuit commodity. Therefore in reaction, I would find something to obsess about. I was a commodity because important Jesuits (Weller and Logan) decreed that I was going to be a high school Latin teacher. Just forget, Casey, that you are a lousy Latin student. You are scheduled to do this, and, by God, that's what your future is.

Then I would obsess about making sense about Aristotle (prime matter and substantial form; yeah, what the fuck!); or Aquinas (the soul is immortal because it is an immaterial substance). No commodity trading in Aristotle or Aquinas since it was only verbiage. I was an empty vessel, waiting for some life to fill me.

Terry Corrigan had a best buddy from his high school years at the diocesan seminary. The guy was now an ordained priest, assigned to St. Augustine's parish in Spokane, Washington. St. Augustine's was a top prize. The guy's name was Reinard Beaver. He was not a Jesuit, but a diocesan priest.

He renews his contact with Terry (remember Terry? The guy who asked me if I liked him?). In no time at all he visits Terry at the Mount. Terry invites me to gather with the two of them for a visit. And I do.

Well, Father Beaver is a real fruit, and I don't feel O.K. about him at all. But Terry is my best friend, and so I groove with the scene.

In a couple of weeks Father Beaver shows up again with his top prize, Chad Mitchell of the soon-to-be famous Chad Mitchell Trio. We all meet in the visitor's area: Terry, Father Beaver, Chad Mitchell, and the hapless Mike Casey from North Dakota. The three of them are relaxed and chatting easily, except for Mike Casey who suffers from a porcupine stuffed up his rear end. But I am polite and civil anyway.

In the next few weeks, I keep Father Beaver in mind, but don't worry about it since just who would I speak to about this anyway?

(I want to tell you that nowadays, years later, I am just fine being around gay men or women. No problem. In fact, I often prefer their company to straight people, who, alas, are often Republican.) It wasn't that Fr. Beaver was a fruit, but that he was a creep.

In a few more weeks, Terry tells me that Beaver is coming again and would I like to accompany Terry and Beaver on a day trip, to say, Grand Coulee Dam, ninety miles west of Spokane. Beaver is taking the two of us out on a date.

I am just a commodity, and do not know how to say "No." Thus, all three of us get in Beaver's new Impala Chevrolet for the drive to Grand Coulee. I sit in the back seat the whole way. Remember the thirteen year old kid in the bunkhouse south of Parshall, North Dakota in Mountrail County in 1948? Remember him at all? Bill Olson on top of me, full humping missionary position in the dark of the Western night?

Well, on the drive back from Grand Coulee, I am expecting the worst.

But the worst does not happen since I am emitting sour vibrations all the way back to Spokane.

Beaver drops Terry and me off at the Mount, and I never hear of him again, ... until 2005, when my sister in Spokane, Patty Buckmaster, sends me a clipping from the Spokesman Review newspaper with names and pictures of the main culprits in the priestly pedophile mess that drove the Spokane Diocese into bankruptcy. Picture number one was Fr. Reinard Beaver himself.

CHAPTER 15: PALL MALLS AND FATHER LEGAULT

What I have to say next may seem complicated since two factors are involved. The first is my addiction to smoking cigarettes. The second is Father Gene LeGault, S.J.

First, the cigarette addiction. The actual problem was not the Marlborough Man, but a pig named Eugene Pacelli. His title was Pope Pius the Twelfth and he had been the spiritual advisor to Adolf Hitler, Heinrich Himmler, the obese Herman Goring, and Joe Goebels. I only mention the top Nazis in the Catholic Party, or is it the top Catholics in the Nazi Party?

Anyway, the ditty is:

Pacelli is a smarty.

He joined the Nazi Party.

Well, in 1955, when the top Nazis had passed beyond this earthly veil, Pius the Pig needed a big distraction from his odious past. Folk are catching on to his villainies. And he must show the world that he is above reproach.

He decrees that no Jesuits can be allowed to smoke cigarettes. In politics, this would be a wedge issue. You know, drive non-smokers against smokers, all in the name of the Greater Glory of God.

This decree was uttered when the Marlborough Man pranced on his horse on the nation's T.V. sets. Many Jesuits were already smokers, puffing entire cartons of Lucky Strikes.

What about those Jesuits already addicted? If they quit the weeds, they would instead have to take up masturbation. The Jesuit General, Father John Baptist Jansens, S.J., himself a fierce masturbator, issued a decree to supplement that of the Pope. It states: "You who are already addicted, and fear the sin of masturbation, well, O.K., just keep puffing. But don't puff in front of the Holy Father. And for God's sake don't masturbate in front of him either." Masturbation and smoking cigarettes, it is believed, both relieve tension, the enervation that all of us in the religious life want to avoid.

I was not a smoker and thought no more about the Pope's decree. But Terry Corrigan often had cigarettes and urged me to try them. I did.

Three puffs later, I am addicted. I will do all I can to get a pack of Pall Malls or Marlboroughs into my pocket. I lift the weeds here and there, when and as I can. Sometimes, Ed Crowley, a lay brother, gives them to me. And so on. In a few months all I can think of is: where, how, when will I get my next smoke? I also despise Pius the Pig and General Jansens.

This filthy habit came to rule my life for the next twenty years.

I study philosophy all day long, and in time, I decide that I need a break. Corrigan is out of cigarettes for the day. Rats! I need a smoke. I've told you I have no free will and am just a Jesuit commodity.

This driving insanity means that I must seek out Jake Bischoff, S.J., a classmate and a very good buddy.

Alas, Jake has no weeds on him but tells me how to get some. He says, "Steal them from Father LeGault." Jake is a realist and very honest about human nature. I do not yet have his honesty. But, please, Jesus Christ, I need a smoke.

To cure cigarette addiction a person must have his lips and tongue cut off. Pius the Twelfth would be very good at this task.

Be patient, please, with my rambling. The unconscious needs much time to get to the point. I am not a machine but I do stand under the Standard of Christ Our Lord (Father Master and Father Toner by my side). But I really need a smoke.

So, who is Father LeGault, S.J.? He is a retired military chaplain from World War II. He was on Eisenhower's staff. He knows all the generals, brigadiers, and colonels. He was one of them. And, of course, they are all fornicators and pederasts.

He is now about sixty years old, and is assigned small parish duties to the north of Spokane, that is, Springdale, Deer Park, Cusick, and points north. He has a car and a pension check from the Army.

Eisenhower is President of the U.S.A. LeGault knows him. He also knows the two U.S. Senators from Washington State, Warren Magnuson and Henry Jackson. These politicos are heavy hitters in Washington, D.C. Father LeGault brings these two worthies to Mount St. Michael's when they are looking to secure even more votes in Eastern Washington. These Senators are Democrats, devoted to bringing the big bucks from Washington, D.C. to Washington State for the likes of Boeing, Grand Coulee Dam, Hanford Nuclear, Kaiser Aluminum.

Father LeGault is well connected. His presence at the Mount means votes for the Senators. To cement this relationship, he arranges to have several of us meet in a small group with the Senators after each gives a talk to the entire community. In the small group we get to ask them questions.

In a different context, Father LeGault asks Jake Bischoff and Mike Casey, neither of us fruits, to drive with him in his Ford station wagon to visit some parishioners north of Spokane. We do as requested. Jake drives; Mike as usual is in the back seat.

The several visits take only about an hour. Then the three of us repair to some tavern for steak and bourbon in Deer Park, Washington (population: 400).

At Mount Saint Michael's, Father LeGault has a room at the end of the first floor corridor. His door is often open and cigarette smoke pours out of it. Often young Jesuit philosophy students step in to chat with him. He speaks about Eisenhower.

His room has a desk close to the door with many current books on it. I remember seeing William B. Fuckley's Man and God at Yale on the desk. Also, there is an overstuffed armchair, a filing cabinet, and a single bed.

On the desk, however, is always a carton of Pall Mall cigarettes. It is open and packages of cigarettes are stashed about the room. The carton is perched on a pile of books, some by William B. Fuckley, and others.

Father LeGault is a very large man, about six feet three inches, not very fat, and bald headed. At the end of the school day about five forty-five p.m. he leaves his room and goes to the community litanies. Afterwards it's supper 'til six forty-five. Then everyone repairs to recreation rooms to watch Huntley and Brinkley.

Jake says, "It's simple. You stand in the shadows at the end of the corridor, where the laundry chute is. You check if he goes to supper, then you slip into his room, lift a pack or two of Pall Malls. Simple. I'll save you a pork chop from the main meal, and we'll go outside, eat, and smoke." Jake had the angles figured. Michael Casey Dum Dum buys the procedure. Jake and Casey are still juveniles. Twenty-three year old juveniles.

I stand in the aforementioned shadows. Is that actually Fr. LeGault going down the corridor to litanies and evening meal? It sure looks like him. I gotta have a smoke with my pork chop.

Fuck it! I'm going in.

I test the door knob and open it quietly, move the door open, and step into the room. Easy now, Mike Casey, the Pall Malls are on the corner of the desk nearest the door. The room is dark.

I step in. Father LeGault says in his best Eisenhower deep voice, "How are you doing, Mike? Come on in."

He knows me and is waiting for someone, maybe me.

Father LeGault is sitting in his overstuffed armchair drinking a scotch and soda, the very drink of the nineteen fifties. In no time at all I have a scotch and soda in my hand, maybe only the third one in my whole life. I start to slurp on it as Father Gene LeGault tells me about his duties on Eisenhower's campaign in North Africa. He mentions Kay Sommersby, Ike's official mistress, and how LeGault and the other colonels had to keep the news of it out of the presidential campaigns. You work for these guys, and you get to have all the scotch and soda you want. What Father LeGault says is interesting. He keeps filling my glass and offering me another Pall Mall.

No other chair is in the room. He says, "Why don't you sit there on the edge of my bed, Mike?"

I do as he says. And I am nearly sloshed by the booze. Can you see where this is going? Sure, so let's get to it.

In no time I'm on my back on his bed, and he asks me if I want a massage.

I utter a "Huh, a whadd?", through slurred speech. I am not a Mickey who can hold his liquor.

Father LeGault has a hand held massage machine, powered by a cord from an electrical outlet. He begins to buzz me with this. Then he suggests that I pull off my tee shirt. A bit later he says, "Loosen your belt so I can massage your abdomen."

By now several glasses of Scotch have seeped into the center of my volitional cortex. I say, "Yeah, sure, it's O.K." He buzzes me some more with the hand held massage machine. Then he drops the electrical unit onto the floor, and crawls on top of me.

His arms are around my neck. LeGault is a big guy, maybe 200 pounds. I am sloshed by the booze. But no force is necessary. All has gone smoothly. Did this happen to Bischoff, to others in need of Pall Malls?

LeGault comes. He grunts a bit. Then he slips to the side of the bed against the wall. He seems to be asleep.

I work out from under him, grab my tee shirt, and head for the door.

The community is still at supper, and I head to my room on the third floor. Wondering. Wondering. Wondering. Did this really happen?

But it did. It happened while I stood under the banner of Christ, smoking a Pall Mall. Sordid. Cheap. Me.

Even though I am a vowed Jesuit holding a sopping wet bag of dog shit, my name is on that bag. Let's not even think about this.

CHAPTER 16: DON'T YOU EVER TOUCH ME AGAIN

The next Jesuit to put his mitts on me was not even a pederast. He was too short to crawl on top of me. He was Fr. Regis Dinky, S.J.

Father Dinky was the Father Minister of the Jesuit Community at Marquette High School in Yakima, Washington. This was a small parish school with perhaps one hundred seventy-five students. The parish was named St. Joseph's. There was a large church, and a grade school.

In 1959 I was assigned there as the main teacher of the freshman class. Thus I was a homeroom teacher. I also coached freshman football, and junior Varsity basketball. Also, I was in charge of the Athletic property room (same as when I was the property manager at Gonzaga High School in 1950-52). I also drove the school bus for the various teams. "Look, Mama, after seven years in the Jesuits, I actually get to drive the bus!"

In the classroom I did well. I taught Latin, English, History, Religion, and Algebra. The students and the parents liked me.

I was not much of a coach and only a mediocre mechanic regarding the school bus. It often broke down.

But I really liked teaching. My mother had been a teacher in a small country school in North Dakota. She taught me to read when I was four years old, and I believed that I inherited her talent as a teacher.

But, the coaching, bus driving, and property room duties always wore me out.

In the previous chapter I stated that at a certain turning point in your life, a key individual can influence your life for the better. This you can always remember and be grateful for. It's as though the person's spirit becomes part of yours.

By the same token, some other individual can disrespect you so deeply that you can go negative. If enough of these negators converge, you become utterly demoralized to the point of not believing that you can make any progress.

Stay with me a bit. I will soon get to my grievance.

Here are some facts. Father Dinky is the chaplain of the high school. He is also the confessor to the Providence Nuns who operate the grade school at St. Joseph's. On Sundays, during the several masses said at St. Joseph's, he puts on a cape, grips a metal sprinkler of holy water, struts up and down the aisles of the main church while flinging the holy water over the parishioners' heads. They love this. This is the entertainment they have paid for. As he does this, he is grinning.

In his office, where the high school lads are supposed to make confession, there is a kneeler next to his desk. On his desk rests a bleached human skull. I think that his mother gave this to him when he made his first communion at the age of six years. He also gives sermons to the lads that it is a mortal sin to use the swimming pool at the Y.M.C.A. The "Y" is a block away. And the "Y" is believed to be a Protestant organization.

As Father Minister in the Jesuit community his main duties are to hand out toothpaste, shaving cream, and cigarettes to those Fathers who have permission to smoke.

I don't have this permission, and so I ask Father Walt Leedale for a pack of weeds. Walt is cool and suave and gives them to me. I smoke them in my room.

After teaching all day, it's coaching junior varsity basketball in the Yakima State Armory. The school does not have its own gymnasium. The custodian of the Armory is a pit bull with a loud voice. He hates me, and orders me to sweep the floor and locker rooms after practice. I perform these menial tasks, after teaching and coaching all day, with a heart full of joy since I am still a Jesuit dum-dum.

Nor does it bother me that the other Jesuits are all back at the residence watching Huntley-Brinkley before sitting down to supper. About this, I am not disgruntled at all. I simply reward myself with the honorary title of "The Hardest Worker in the Marquette High stockyard."

It happens that sometimes I don't make the beginning of supper at six p.m. The bus breaks down, whatever. I return to the residence, go directly to my room, remove my clothes, and put on my heavy wool Jesuit black cassock. Then I return to the dining room.

Perhaps, supper is half finished. But others have kept an empty chair for me next to the entrance to the room.

Now, here's the deal: I often push my sleeves up near my elbows, so itchy is the heavy wool of my cassock. I sit and begin to shovel the grub down my gullet.

It also happens that Father Dinky is sometimes also late and swoops in behind me. As I slurped down the split pea soup and crackers, he passed my right arm, flesh exposed. The manly black hair on my arm is swanking in plain sight.

Father Regis Rat-face cannot resist this sight. His fingers reach down and pinch the hair on my arm. He pulls the hair and this startles me.

I ask you: has anyone ever done this to you? Or something similar? And how did you react?

Yeah, exactly. You jumped up from your chair and split pea soup. You reach out to grab his hands and fingers. This is reflex. You don't have to meditate on this. This is what happens. Maybe even words are exchanged.

Dinky squeals, "I told you before not to expose your arms. Don't do it anymore."

The Rules of Jesuit Modesty, my-oh-my! Such a scandal!

I attempted to slide my chair back from the table. But the chair jammed on the rug. My motion is upward but clumsy. My right arm swings out and backward, and just misses this Professed Father, with a special vow of obedience to the pope. He squeals.

The dozen or so Jesuits in the dining room see and hear this. Some think that I have actually bashed him. Don't I wish!

Did you know that it is a mortal sin to hit a cleric? Canon Law forbids it. Even a real dinky cleric.

Later that evening Father Superior and the pastor of the entire parish, asks me into his room. He fidgets in his chair, can hardly make eye contact. He alerts me not to pester Father Dinky, the poor little chicken-shit.

Not as dangerous as the Waltz of the Butcher Knife Jesuits. But the theme is the same: Mike Casey is the designated smuck.

A few days go by while I steam about this. Then one evening after driving the bus to Toppenish for a basketball game, I return to my room. I reach for my cigarettes. But they are not there. Instead, a note is on my desk. It reads:

"Mr. Casey, you must see me in my room in the morning."

It was signed by Father Regis Dinky of the Society of those real dinky sunken-cheeked pig-fuckers.

What kind of guy searches your room looking for an excuse to humiliate you? Especially when he had every opportunity to approach you in plain sight. Exactly! He is a coward. He doesn't have the balls to go face to face with you. He has studied Canon Law and needs this cheezy canonical protocol to cover his tracks.

The next morning I go to his room. Remember that demented vow of obedience I took? What I had experienced as black, while the Professed Fathers say is white? Remember the teenager who gave up his free-will, and even worse cannot figure out how to find it again? Yeah! That idealistic kid? Sicut cadaver (like a dead man!).

I enter his room and sit opposite him. On his desk is that goddam bleached human skull.

He begins to chew my ass about the weeds. He says, "Father Provincial has not given you permission to smoke, has he?" He says this like a lawyer who asks questions only when he knows the enfeebling answer.

On his desk there is also a metal letter opener. He is a Professed Father and can't just tear the letter open, as the rest of us groundlings do. But he keeps the opener on his side of the desk. Really, is he afraid of me?

Next he hammers me about the cassock sleeves transgression. I say, "But my arms itch from the wool." He ignores my answer.

Then his eyes narrow, he places both hands on the desk, leans forward a bit. His lips tighten and he says, "I think you should really consider if this Jesuit life is for you."

This is like a knife stuck into my heart. The little cocksucker really means this.

I go into a bit of a shock and don't react. Sicut a real cadaver.

What I finally say is: "Don't you ever touch me again."

He mutters about the rule of Modesty, i.e., no bare arms allowed.

"Don't you ever touch me again."

He tries to let this go by. But I say it again, "Don't you ever touch me again."

He squirms a bit. Then, I give our sonny boy another shot. "Don't you ever touch me again." My voice is very tight but I don't choke.

He gets his balance back and says, "I am the prefect of discipline in this Jesuit residence. No more smoking without permission and keep your sleeves down at the dining table."

I say it again: "Don't you ever touch me again."

My throat and stomach are constricted.

I stand up. He says, "You should think hard about leaving the Jesuits."

"Don't you ever touch me again!"

He was still sitting when I left his room. He was holding the letter opener.

What he has said to me is against all the instruction that Father Master had instilled in me.

Leaving the Jesuits can only be a matter of conscience between me and the Provincial of the Order (and even the Provincial cannot give you the boot). No Superior would ever dare to tell a guy to leave the Order. You actually have to request the Order's permission to leave. And only Father General in Rome can give such permission. But even he can't give a guy the boot.

And Dinky is not Father Provincial. He is only the prefect of discipline and has, by the rules of the Jesuit Order, no competence in matters of conscience (the "internal forum"). He should stick to handing out toothpaste and shaving cream.

Dinky's stunt really demoralized me. But as my first year of teaching developed, I came to some resolve. It was that I really liked teaching and did well in the classroom. Teaching was my life as an intelligent person seeking a life of spirit.

Inevitably, I despised Dinky and others like him (there would be others). The rules of modesty, as well as other rules, well, I came to just not let them bother me. And I continued to smoke cigarettes.

Me telling Dinky, "Don't you ever touch me again," didn't actually liberate me from the noxious strictures of the vow of obedience. But it did break the spell and gave me some breathing room.

Dinky's display of the bleached skull was only the surface of his real ambition. What he really wanted was to be a fully licensed exorcist.

An exorcist's job is to cast out devils. For this he needs Father Provincial's permission as well as the local bishop's. This takes the form of an actual license. To acquire one of these, the exorcist-to-be needs practice. This is very dangerous work since it is a well-known fact that the devil can leave the body of the original victim and enter the body of the exorcist himself. I am not making this up! All this is in the bible. Christ cast out devils. Father Dinky casts out devils. He then fallaciously concludes that he himself is Christ. Good luck with that one, Dinky!

Really, why was Dinky searching my room? Maybe he's checking the sheets for stray spermatozoa. Or is he looking for a really big devil, one condemned by Pope Pius the Pig in his encyclical "Numquam Puffendum Pall Mall."

Hell is the home of devils. The flames there cause much noxious smoke. Where there is smoke, there is a devil. Where there is cigarette smoke, there is a cigarette devil. Cigarette smoke emerges from Mike Casey's room. Therefore there is a devil in his room. And Dinky must exorcise that devil. That devil is Mike Casey.

While I was driving the bus to and from Toppenish, Dinky fortifies himself with prayer and fasting. He hugs his bleached human skull, burns some incense, nails a dead rat above my door, and enters my room.

Ah hah! The evidence of devil worship: a package of Pall Malls. Like Judith holding the head of Holofernes, blood dripping onto the floor, Dinky takes photos of the gristly scene and writes up a story for the National Enquirer.

After the "Don't you ever touch me again" encounter, Dinky got in a parish car and drove to Pasco, Washington. You know what that means?

Pasco, Washington is where Janice the Witch lived. It is true that Janice was not comely, as the bristles growing out of the side of her nose indicated. But she was proficient at sorcery.

Father Dinky reached into his skull (the bleached one he carried on these missions) and pulled out two twenty dollar bills and laid them on Janice's table.

He said, "You know what I want."

Janice said, "A hex on Michael Casey, S.J.?"

Dinky whispered, "Yes. And right now."

Janice took some dried thistles, placed them into an empty can of Valvoline, soaked them with lighter fluid. Then she tossed a Tarot card on the mess, lit a match, and tossed it into the can. The flames were brief but did the job. Dinky coughed from the fumes and Janice slipped the twenties into her purse where she kept her rosary. Janice mumbled an incoherent prayer. Then the deed was done.

As Fr. Dinky got up to leave, Janice again reached into her purse, and retrieved a holy card. On it was the picture of Pope Pius the Pig. She had also written on the back of it her personal phone number. Dinky took the card and left.

The hex was upon me from that day forward. I continued to chew on Dinky's warning: "You should think hard about leaving the Jesuits."

CHAPTER 17: THE BISHOPRICK IN THE PARKING LOT

As the school year of 1959 to 1960 drew to a close, a terrible jolt hit the entire Jesuit community of Marquette High. The local bishop (not himself a Jesuit) the Reverend Bishoprick William Daugherty told the Jesuits all to leave his diocese. He says, "I mean right now!"

We are all to just get out, and his own diocesan priests will take over. The only Jesuits to stay are the parish priests at St. Joseph's Church.

He has his own new Central Catholic High School and he wants no competition from the Jesuits. Besides, Marquette High is just a block from downtown and is very valuable property.

But there is an even deeper reason. There is a strong Marquette Boosters Club of businessmen who have over several years raised a large wad of cash to build a new athletic complex a few blocks from the school. Daugherty wants this money for his own purposes. The Kingdom of Christ can go in more than one direction, you know.

Hey, Brothers and Sisters, be alert now, because I'm about to leap forward in time. But I will soon return to my squalid fate as a displaced Jesuit teacher from Marquette High in Yakima, Washington.

In 1965 I was ordained a priest. The Jesuit High Command assigned me to St. Joseph's parish for that summer. On weekdays I say the eight o'clock Mass. I step out of the rectory and start to walk across the parking lot to the back door of the church. Just then three guys in clerical suits emerge from the church door and begin strutting to their flashy Cadillac. Two of these are obvious flunkies of the Bishoprick William Daugherty. The latter is dressed in bishoprickly splendor. You know, black suit and crimson red vest. A gold chain with a gold crucifix hangs from his neck. His shoes are polished and the early morning sunlight glistens off them. The crimson, the black, and the gold broadcast Daugherty's importance. He is nearly impressive.

We moving closer now, and he recognizes me. "Ah! Father Casey, welcome to St. Joseph's."

I am staring into the abyss of hypocrisy. Significant protocol is required of me. I hesitate. Should I run and hide? But, no. My personal Holy Ghost tells me not to.

But, then the Holy Ghost's chief assistant, St. Michael the Archangel, flicks on the light of truth inside my noggin. This is a taboo, I am about to smash. Deo gracias, St. Michael.

The canonical protocol is that I am to drop to one knee and kiss the episcopal ring. He will extend his hand. A knobby finger with a golden ring on it will reach out to my sycophantic lips. And I must abase myself again. Not as bad as LeGault on top of me, but in the same category.

Ahhg! I want to wretch.

And where has that finger been lately?

Well, just fuck it, I can't do that!

He sticks his claw out. On it is a massive gold ring. The morning sunlight lights it up like a cheezie Christmas tree.

In the parking lot I teeter between good and evil. Should I transcend both? Nietzsche would be proud of me. Then again, Saint Michael the Archangel, the Supreme Pragmatist, whispers in my ear, "Come on, dummy, just shake his hand, you know, just press the flesh." Good old St. Michael.

I reach out, grab his claw, shake it well. Now, here's the good part. I don't let go. I pump some more. This is his hand, not his prick, I am pumping.

I say, "How you doing? Good to see you. I'm glad to be here for the summer. Isn't this weather great? I might even go fishing later today. Maybe come back with a nice steelhead. Golly, wouldn't that be swell?"

I am still pumping. Small talk comes out of my mouth. And I mean every word of it. I hock up a hint of an Irish brogue "...in me voice, and sure, ain't I a rascal!"

I'm reading Daugherty as a latter-day Mickey from, say, the mid-West. I am in the middle of smashing a Taboo, and I gotta finish in good style.

Daugherty is transfixed. By now my inhibitions are wearing off, so I put both my mitts on his ring hand, in case he tries to bolt from my two-fisted pumping.

Now I have a golden thought of my own. I say, "Say, Bishop Daugherty, did you know that my paternal grandmother was a Daugherty herself. Yeah, Margaret Daugherty. She was born in Shakopee, Minnesota. You betcha! That's right outside of Minneapolis. I was named after her brother, my dad's uncle. His name was Michael Daugherty. There's a lot of Daugherty in me. Black Irish, you know. Boy, oh, Boy! These Minnesota roots go back a long way."

"Hey, yourself now, ye ever been to Minnesota? Grand Catholics there, just grand!"

I'm still pumping. Daugherty is starting to shift around on his two polished black boots, even turns his head towards one of the flunkies. His eyes say, "Free me from this MAD Mickey!"

The flunky says, "Your Excellency, we have another appointment. Shall we get into the car to leave?"

It's not everyday an episcopal TABOO is violated there in the Yakima Valley of Washington State, there among the Red Delicious apples blossoming in the orchards, there where mad Mickeys roam the church parking lots.

Daugherty himself is still speechless, pulls back a little bit.

"Oh say, I almost forgot. I have a cousin named William Daugherty. Yeah...Willy, that's it,...Willy Daugherty. Isn't that a great name? I think he had to go to jail for a while."

I drop his hand, and step back, still facing the Bishoprick.

"And another thing, could you say a prayer for the Daugherty family in Minnesota? They would just love it.

"Have a nice day, good luck, and Erin go Blahh!"

I turn away and walk into the church to start Mass.

The dimwit is still standing there, staring at his hand. He's checking to see if his golden ring is still on his finger.

CHAPTER 18: IF THEY THINK YOU'RE AN ASSHOLE, WELL, YOU'RE AN ASSHOLE

Back now to the spring of 1960 when Daugherty gave the Jesuits the boot. At the end of the school year of 1960, there was then a surplus of Jesuits on the teaching market in the Oregon Province. Thus, the Jesuit high command scatters us to the far corners of the Jesuit Schools of the Province.

Whenever there is a labor surplus, the value of the individual laborer sinks even lower. That means I am worth next to nothing, and therefore am assigned to teach freshman Latin at Seattle Prep, the 'C' and 'D' classes.

For me, this is a real blow. It is as though a special card has been pinned to the province bulletin board, announcing "Mike Casey,

S.J., M.A. in Philosophy, is a dung beetle in the Jesuit shit heap. Please pray for him."

Seattle Prep is the premier Jesuit High School in the province. The Jesuits assigned to that citadel of learning on the north slope of Capitol Hill, overlooking Lake Union and the University of Washington, are thought to be the elite high school teachers in the province. And most of them are. Yet this class distinction applies only to the 'A' and 'B' classes, and especially for the juniors and seniors. The 'C' and 'D' levels, especially among the freshmen, are for those dummies whose parents can afford to pay the steep elitist tuition at Seattle Prep. Prep just reeks of class distinction.

I am not expected to teach the lads in the 'C' and 'D' classes anything. However, I am expected to keep firm discipline over this high testosterone gang with middling academic potential. None of this is explained to me in so many words but is implied in the assignment itself.

The principal of the school is Father Dick Seaver, S.J. He never once says squat to me, not even a letter to me about what he expects from my vowed labor. This is good since it is immediately clear to me that I am a non-entity at Seattle Prep, and therefore can have no illusions about my superfluous calling as a teacher.

Father Seaver never talks to anyone on the faculty unless there's trouble. Then he shows his skill at chewing ass.

Father Seaver is very tall and athletic. Seattle Prep is indeed the very school he graduated from as a star basketball player twenty years before. He is unaware that times and sensibilities have changed. He is determined to keep Seattle Prep as it was in 1940.

But mainly, he's very depressed. It's all over his face and his voice. At the time, depression was never spoken of, especially among Jesuits. Why speak of it or seek relief since we all stand under the banner of Christ the King?

Father Seaver's anger at his life of vowed non-fucking is palpable. This life was inflicted upon him by his family (his older brother is also a Jesuit, and there was also a nun in the family). Also his mother and father still live in the ancestral home atop Capitol Hill.

As principal of Seattle Prep he has not managed to leave home or childhood. Wouldn't this depress anyone?

He leaves the school building every day at the last bell. He drives his car to the top of Capitol Hill in Seattle (Seattle Prep is at the north end of the Hill). There he spends the afternoon and early evening visiting his pals from his own high school days. What a jolly time they must have had.

He rarely eats supper with the Jesuit community. It's obvious that he hates his job and cannot stand being around Jesuits.

We the rank and file talk about him only in terms of: when is he gonna crack? By the way, do you think there's anything to the view that depression can be infectious? I think I'm starting to catch it at Seattle Prep.

Father Seaver has decreed that there can be no talking by the students once they enter the building at 8 a.m. Mike Casey, the central non-entity at Seattle Prep, is given the job of enforcing this unnatural condition in the hallways where the freshmen and sophomores have classrooms. Thus I start the teaching day as a disciplinarian even before I begin Latin class.

This duty is completely against my nature. I don't like it one bit. Sometimes Father Seaver comes out of his office and sternly tells me that there is too much talking going on. He has me confused with the Nazi guard Ivan the Terrible at Treblinka. I am not Ivan and resent this unnatural guard duty.

As hallway enforcer, my job is to enforce this unnatural rule. The doors open at 8 a.m., and I stride up and down the hallway, telling the lads, "No talking. Be quiet. Didn't you hear what I said! No talking."

These lads are fourteen and fifteen years old, and naturally hate me for all of this. Indeed, I begin to hate myself. By the time the bell rings for classes to begin at 8:30 I am in a lather about the lads and myself.

In this assignment as a teacher and disciplinarian at Seattle Prep I can only fail! I snarl a lot. Also I become sarcastic and abusive to the lads whose parents have spent much money for their sons to have a Jesuit education.

You've heard this so many times: the Jesuit philosophy of education is to teach the sons of those wealthy and prominent Catholic families, who, in turn, will "influence" the course of society. It is the Jesuit version of the trickle-down economics of the establishment (Republicans!). The sick part of this is that, this is true at Prep. And the entire community of Jesuits at Seattle Prep form a lock-step battalion to ensure that there are no dissenting voices to this orthodoxy. The motto at Prep is: we teach only the elite. I hate the place.

Hey, Mike, why don't you just leave the Jesuits altogether? My answer is: Gee! I never thought of that. Besides, my mother is still alive.

For two years at Seattle Prep, I juggled two problems at the same time. The light I had available to me to solve these two problems was quite dim since they were developmental problems.

The first was that the Jesuits indicated, at least by deed, that there was no function for me to even be there at Seattle Prep. I was surplus, and the Jesuits might as well have said, "Mike, we have no use for you here."

The second was my own character as an apprentice bully.

Let me give you an appreciation of the second. You've seen it already when I spoke of my chores as disciplinarian over the freshman and sophomores in the hallways, and how I begin the teaching day with a snarl on my lips. Between the hallways and Latin I come across as an asshole. I don't dispute this perception of me. The perception is correct but, in my opinion, it is not who I am. Like Richard Nixon who felt compelled to proclaim, "Well, I'm not a crook," I want to proclaim to the lads that "I am not an asshole." That would really go over big with the lads!

On this level you just can't bullshit young people. And I never tried. But, even so, that is how they did perceive me. I received feedback from other scholastics and priests on the faculty that I was verging on the edge of bullydom.

It's the place and me. There's not much to like in either. Infantile and adolescent stuff has been buried in me and is now beginning to rise to the surface. Some of it is not pleasant, especially this bully business.

And you know how I feel about the bully himself, the very busy Joe!

Other members of the Prep faculty are fully certified bullies, like the school principal himself, Richard Seaver, S.J. Also there are various assistant football coaches who delight in terrorizing the lads. The entire faculty gossips about various students that they all just hate. I join in, and feel rotten about it. Because, after all, just who am I, to look down on lads who are perfectly natural adolescents since I am myself only a late blooming adolescent, even if I don't know it.

No one at Seattle Prep actually uses the word "bully" since that would indict the entire school. The entire matter festers inside of me.

Is it true?

I begin to fear that it is. Indeed once I was at the bus depot in downtown Seattle. I was waiting to pick up my father and mother who were coming from Spokane to visit me for the weekend.

I stood at the entrance to wait for the bus. I recognized a few feet away from me a Seattle Prep student. He was talking to another teenager. Neither were members of my classes. I heard him say, clearly and distinctly, "That guy is the worst teacher at Prep." It was clearly said for my benefit.

My gorge swelled and I wanted to strangle him. But you know how shame works. I swallowed his disrespect for me, and lived for another day. But, God!, it hurt.

At Marquette I had grooved with most of the students. But at Prep I could not identify any who thought of me as cool. Prepsters did not care if you are doing a great job of teaching Latin or English. If they think you're an asshole, well...that's it...the verdict is in: You're an asshole.

It was at Seattle Prep that I began to distinguish my religious vocation (a Jesuit) from my spiritual vocation (a teacher, a teacher of Latin, English, History, and later, Philosophy).

I had hopes of making my mark as a premiere home room teacher. But the Jesuits had other plans for me. Those plans do not include Mike Casey drinking from the bowl of excellence.

For example, at Marquette, I was a coach and bus driver, but my heart was in classroom teaching. At Prep I am neither a coach nor a bus driver. I am a Latin teacher at a level where I can only fail. And what retard aspires to be a disciplinarian?

Behind me, and within me, is my mother. Her spirit is the form of my desire to be a teacher, an ideal that I have never relinquished, then or now. It is what it is.

This is an illustration of what I mean as a spiritual life. My spirit comes from my mother. No two ways about it. And those who knew me then and now would never think of me as a mama's boy.

My mother taught me to read before I went to school. She used the phonics method, and read from the Quaker Oats cereal box and the Sears and Roebuck catalogue. She was a teacher in a country school in Mountrail County, North Dakota. There are people around today who still remember her, back there and even out here on the West Coast. Her last teaching job in North Dakota was in 1929. Brothers and sisters, never underestimate the force of a teacher and the power of the spirit.

The teaching part of my Jesuit vocation is very personal. Were it not for my desire to be a classroom teacher I just would not be in the Jesuits at all. I do have a spiritual life (teaching and reading), as distinct from a religious life.

The latter is just too stupid to speak of. At Seattle Prep I keep quiet about this dichotomy since no Jesuit superior wants to hear of the spiritual yearning of a mad Mickey.

Remember the two problems I spoke of some pages back: one is my character as an emerging bully, and the other that the Jesuits had no actual function for me as a teacher.

It is now time to discuss the second problem: that is, how empty the Jesuit agenda actually is, regarding teaching young people any life of the spirit (and I don't mean the Holy Spirit, whoever that is).

CHAPTER 19: THE "DIRTY GIRLS" HOME

The emptiness of my two years at Seattle Prep is well illustrated by my assignment as sacristan of the community.

The sacristan is the guy or nun who sets out the priestly linens for the many masses that the priests will say the next morning. It is understood that this is "women's" work. Since no women are allowed inside the Jesuit residence, I become a pseudo-woman. This assignment is almost as humiliating as taking the flagellatio. Has some Jesuit hierarch pissed in my soup bowl?

There are four small chapels and one main chapel. The priest stuff must be laid out just so. After the masses this must all be put away. I also change the altar clothes often. In addition I vacuum the rugs on the chapel floors. The next day it's the same goddam procedure.

To qualify as sacristan, a guy must be either a mindless drudge, or at least willing to become one. Thus far, the students think I'm an asshole or a bully, and the Jesuits think I'm a mindless drudge. I ask the Holy Ghost: what is there in this for me? The Holy Ghost keeps his opinion to himself. There will be no help from him.

Once a week I gather all this altar linen and priestly stuff and take them to the House of the Good Shepherd. This convent and others like it are referred to by all Catholics world-wide as the "dirty girls" home. What is shameful is not the young women who are housed there until they give birth to their babies but that the label "dirty girls home" is used openly. No individual shames herself or himself. Shame is dished out on an individual from social mechanisms more powerful than any authority.

The young women there, mostly adolescents, it is said, have had unwanted pregnancies. After their babies have been given up for adoption ("taken away?"), most of these adolescents must stay in the House of the Good Shepherd and work in the laundry in order to pay off their debt of room and board. Does the thought of indentured servitude now enter your mind?

The laundry there does all the linen for the entire Archdiocese. At first I do not understand the economics of the place. But in time I will.

A nun is in charge of the laundry. She supervises the young women who operate the machines. I deliver this week's used linen and pick up last week's newly laundered linen.

At first I am mainly concerned with my own place in this abyss, how much I resent my assignment. I have taken vows of chastity, poverty, and obedience...to do this? In fact I am just a delivery boy hauling laundry from one place to another.

The Jesuit administration at Seattle Prep have hired lay persons to teach English or French, or Algebra, and to coach sports. Good for these lay teachers. The impression I get is that the Jesuits have no need of me as a teacher.

Why can't they also hire a delivery boy to cart the laundry back and forth? Perhaps in time they will ask me to sweep the hallways in the school, mow the grass on the lawn. Maybe I can change the oil in Father Superior's Ford Edsel. I could do this. Yeah, why not? Maybe even polish his shoes.

I begin to catch on to the Jesuit economy. It will in time become obvious that they don't need me. So, just why am I here?

I drive Seattle Prep's station wagon into the parking lot of the "dirty girls" home. I pull up to the loading dock. The entire Archdiocese of Seattle sends laundry there. But I am the only male I ever see there, certainly the only cleric. I do this every Wednesday when all the diocesan priests are playing golf.

I crawl out and lift the laundry out. Then I ring a bell. The door opens, and a nun appears from inside. I say, "I'm from Seattle Prep."

She says, "O.K., Father, haul the stuff in." Young women inside are operating ironing machines, while others are folding priest stuff into piles, and placing them into baskets.

These young women are the "dirty girls." I feel much tension in the room. Is this my tension or theirs? All seems both strange and obscure.

After a couple of weeks two or three of the women smile at me and say hello. Some even wave to me.

The strange and obscure tension is at work.

After several laundry trips to the "dirty girls" house, it dawns on me that the tension is that these young women are prisoners, and can't get out of the deal.

Just like Me!

I can't see that there is any spiritual difference between my own bottom-level Jesuit role, and the role of the young women (and the nun herself) in the "dirty girls" home.

When I deliver the laundry, I feel completely out of my element. I don't know the names of any of the young women in the laundry, nor even the nun's name. Remember what I told you about sexual ignorance? Well, it extends even to knowing the names of these young women. These are the only women I have been around since I was sixteen years old at the Hillyard swimming pool. Dare I wave back at them?

The nun calls me "Father." In time one of the girls asked me if I am a priest. I say, "No, I'm a Jesuit." She has no idea what a Jesuit is, and gives me a funny look. Indeed, I agree with her reaction since even I now believe that Jesuits are "funny."

The next week the same girl follows me to the station wagon at the loading dock. Another girl is with her. They want to tell me something.

She says, "One time me and Mandy ran away from this place. We got all the way to Tacoma. Then the cops got us and made us come back here. Hey, you know, we're gonna try it again if we get the chance."

I mutter a "Yeah, I gotta get back to Prep." I jumped into the station wagon and backed out with the laundry.

But the wheels inside my noggin were spinning a fantasy. "I'll drive the station wagon back to the loading dock, tell them to jump in, and I'll drive them to Tacoma. They will be grateful to me."

"Attention: All State Police: There is an All Points Bulletin for Michael Humbert Humbert, S.J. He's wanted for kidnapping some teenage girls. Their names are Mandy and Lolita. He's not armed. But he suffers from delusions."

I wanted to be a hero, help them out, cherish them.

I drove back to Prep, put away the priest stuff, and took a long cold shower.

I wasn't thinking of leaving the Jesuits, but if I did leave, why not leave with a couple of young women who needed a lift? But I know full well that I can not help anyone since I am a Jesuit. How can I help these girls if I can't even help myself?

I am demented with frustration and disappointment. It took many cold showers to persevere the rest of that school year. Sexual ignorance is not easily showered off in a healthy Mickey.

The lads that I teach in the "D" class are from well-off or even wealthy families. This is the Jesuit plan for conquering the world: to influence the elite, Jesuits begin by teaching the children of the elite. A Jesuit must have faith that these elite will in time lift up the working classes by their heroic example and good works. Yeah, sure.

In effect, this means that I am teaching only Republicans. You know how I feel about that.

The prevailing attitude at Prep, both in the student body and among the faculty, reeks of big bucks and the names of prominent citizens of Seattle. I have little in common with them. They are not my kind at all. I feel the friction.

One effect on me from the disparity between teaching at Prep and realizing the plight of the young women at the "dirty girls" home is that I begin to actively dislike my Jesuit vocation. This is the "religious" side of my life. But the "spiritual" side of my life, which derives from my mother's example as a teacher, is intrinsic to me. That is, if I could get out from the Jesuit harness, I would get a job teaching with the public schools. I joined the Jesuits because I wanted some status in the world as an educated person. I also joined because I wanted to be a teacher. Well, it turns out, doesn't it, that the Jesuit Order has no need for me as a teacher. Also, what education is necessary to be a sacristan (a pseudo-woman) or a laundry delivery boy?

This is how I have my situation sized up at the end of my second year of teaching.

CHAPTER 20: IS THAT KITTY KELLY IN THE BLUE DRESS?

At the end of May, 1961, the summer status is posted on the community bulletin board. It is a report as to where various Jesuits will be stationed for the months of June, July, and August. It states that Michael Casey will be teaching philosophy for three months at Gonzaga University in Spokane.

This is how God's Will is manifested to me. I can hardly believe my luck. I realize immediately that my sponsor is Father John Leary, S.J., the Dean at Gonzaga. He has by-passed Father William, the Prick, Weller, S.J., and just decreed that I was his hoplite for the summer. I had no inkling that this assignment was in the works. It also reflected the fact that my mother was a practical nurse in an Old Folks Home in Spokane. One of her patients was Father Leary's bed-ridden mother. This is again the presence of my mother behind my desire to be a teacher. The Holy Spirit has been of no help to me. In fact he was still called the Holy Ghost. But my mother's spirit is at work. Don't ask me how, but it is there.

Father Leary sends me a note stating that I will be teaching Rational Psychology. Rational Psychology is not psychology at all. It is not based on any science. It is the philosophy of Aquinas and Aristotle applied to human beings; mostly it is about the "soul". Recall that the word "psychology" comes from the Greek word for "soul" (psyche).

The word "rational" in the Thomistic and Jesuit vocabulary means that it is not revealed. Thus, there was revealed theology as distinct from rational theology (what can be established by reason alone).

Rational Psychology's main engine is that the soul and the body are distinct as substances. The body dies and is thrown into the dirt. But the soul lives on since it is incorporeal. Can here you foresee the crude hand of theology subverting the realm of reason in philosophy? And while I'm at this, let me bring in the Inquisition with its bonfires: it's o.k. to burn heretics and, of course Jews, since the body is just a sluggish thing, whereas the soul, being incorporeal, is not flammable. It merely disappears into the ether, never to be seen again except late at night in haunted houses. Aquinas never says that the soul is your spirit, but only that it is not physical or combustible.

But you object, as folk always do when Aquinas has the floor: If the soul is not combustible, what about the fires of hell, where the souls of the damned are banished? and presumably burned for eternity?

Aquinas says, "Well, this does get kinda tricky. But don't get yourself sent to hell in the first place. Remember that a good canon lawyer can get you off if you have the right connections."

For eight weeks in the summer of 1961 I spoke this dreck to young men and women.

You want to ask: Casey, did you not have any self-respect? Of course I didn't because I didn't have a self, let alone respect for it. Have you forgotten about all that self-flagellation (literally) and the cras catenellae stunt, and Joe Logan's black is white knife in the ribs, or that bag of dog shit I carried out of LeGault's room during the season of humping, or Regis Dinky's humiliation of me during his sheet-inspection of my room.

Rational Psychology fits right in here, and so I endured.

The positive part of this assignment is that there are a number of young women in the class. Some are very attractive and I wonder if

I'm in the right business. One in particular was Kitty Kelly. She later became well known as the author of biographies of famous people, like Jackie Kennedy, Frank Sinatra, and the British Royals. She usually wore a light blue dress which accentuated her narrow waist and ample bosom. I thought about her a lot. She wrote down everything I said. This made me nervous since most of what I said was Thomistic gibberish. But she wrote it down anyway.

Well, enough of this name dropping.

Father Leary often came to my room in the dormitory. He came to instruct me about teaching. But usually he would just barge in after knocking. He made me nervous. I really wasn't sure about him. What did he really want?

At the end of the summer he drove me and a couple of other Jesuit scholastics, Gary Grief and Gordon Moreland, to a fancy restaurant. We ate and chatted. He paid the bill and then we all got into the car. As usual I was in the back seat. Before we drive off, he takes three envelopes out of his suit coat and gives one to each of us. We open them. Inside mine was seventy-five dollars. This made me very apprehensive. He's paying us in cash.

This made me think about his motives since this procedure goes against my understanding of the vow of poverty.

But the money burned a hole in my pocket. In the next few weeks I bought some books I wanted to read. I also bought a whole carton of cigarettes (no more breaking into LeGault's room for me!). But when I got back to Seattle Prep for the next school year, I turned the remainder over to Father Gene Toner, who was the Minister of Prep. I didn't tell him where it came from. This act alone proves that I am a prude about the vow of poverty, and a real ninny with no self-respect, and a complete Loyola dumdum. Will I ever snap out of it?

I didn't catch on to Father Leary until seven years later, when my father, Matt Casey, gave me the real dope: the Spokane cops descended on Gonzaga University, snap the cuffs on Leary, and have him out of town within the hour. By then, he has been promoted to President of the University. It seems that he has forced himself on several young male students while on road trips to alumni gatherings (he was known as a great fundraiser). Eventually the young men turn him in to the police.

This quick departure from Spokane was not reported to the papers. It's a replay of the 1951 Toulouse pederasty scene. No one knows what's going on until thirty years later when both stories are printed in Northwest newspapers.

You have to hand it to the Jesuits. They can really keep the lid on tight. And of course, the payout money for the victims is sitting in the Jesuit savings account earning interest for thirty or forty years.

So, why did I feel so strange about the seventy-five dollars back in 1961? What was it for? It wasn't for services rendered since I had no contract with the school.

It was for my loyalty and silence in case anything came to light if I was asked any incriminating questions about Leary's pederasty.

I didn't understand this then. But I do now. And I want you to appreciate my opinion about the Church and the Jesuits.

CHAPTER 21: FATHER JACK CONFESSES THE MADAMS

My stint at Gonzaga University in 1961 led me to think that I might have some value to the Oregon Province as an esteemed professor of Rational Psychology. Will these delusions ever cease?

When I returned in the fall of 1961 to Seattle Prep, my delusions evaporated as I resumed my deliveries to the House of the Good Shepherd. Also, the superior of Prep, Father Jack Murphy, approached me and said, "Say, Mike, why don't you help out our freshman football coach, Jim Harney? He's swamped with it all. He could use some assistance."

His condescending Excellence, Father Jack Murphy. He calls me "Mike", and this means he's at his manipulating best. Before this, he had never made even eye-contact with me.

Thus I am the assistant to the assistant of the freshman football team. The entire fall season passes in a fog. But I do remember dressing in cleats and refereeing football games. Parents show up for these games, and do they ever resent my many bad calls. And so do the football coaches. What bowl of viper piss have I supped from?

I am in the wrong place. Am I also in the wrong life? By virtue of the brainwashing or mind control that I had undergone in the Novitiate, I lack all self-knowledge. What I do know is that I hate everything at Prep: football, laundry, disciplinarian of the school's hallways, no grooving with the students, confessing my endless streams of stray spermatozoa (disguised as "impure thoughts"), the Republican class distinctions in the student body; and also, have I mentioned to you the drunken orgies in the Jesuit community itself?

Every Friday after school is out for the week, Father Minister opens the bottles of premium scotch, and nearly all of us get smashed, just shit-faced under the banner of Loyola. Booze is the intermittent reinforcement for the vain stupidities of the three vows: Get drunk and sleep it off and then grin and bear it for another week. In one of these orgies, I blacked out. I don't mean passed out. I mean, blacked out.

Especially during my second year at Seattle Prep, my simmering class resentment began to center around Father Jack Murphy, S.J., the Father Superior of the entire Jesuit Bund in Seattle.

He had made his reputation as a terrific English teacher. And he was a great public speaker. Sometimes he was even eloquent. Unlike Toulouse he is not a pederast but he is an elitist. And, boy, oh, boy! is he ever hot shit. Father Dinky was just a warmed over turd. But Jack Murphy, S.J. is indeed hot shit.

You look at him and you are reminded of the American Bald Eagle. Except the eagle is not actually bald. Father Joe Logan tried to just blow you away with his self-importance. Murphy, on the other hand, projects superiority: the superiority of a commanding officer whom all the troops plain hate. Indeed, it is impossible to imagine anyone actually liking Murphy.

He is both superior and pious. I am sure that he is Irish, but it is beyond my imagination that any Irishman could be so sterile. I, for one, simply cannot think of him as suffering from a throbbing hard-on of any duration. Not for nothing is he named Father Superior.

He was appointed to this position in order to raise money. That's it, folks: he is a Jesuit, and he wants your money. He has established a building fund to build a new school and faculty residence. This is his cover for the A.M.D.G. side of the Jesuit Kingdom.

The Jesuits have a reputation as great teachers. They are also known as great fundraisers. And they can be great assholes. Father J.V. Murphy combined all three.

He also wants to be known as a premier confessor to nuns. You can read about this in many history books, how convents of nuns preferred Jesuits as their confessors because of their intellect. "Wu, wu."

Murphy wants big donations. He understands that to get the big dough he must go to where the money is. Thus he appoints himself as confessor to the convent of the Madams of the Sacred Heart. No young woman wishing to follow in the footsteps of the Lord is allowed to join the Madams of the Sacred Heart unless her parents are very wealthy and can come up with a giant dowry for the young woman.

These nuns (excuse me, Madams) are the elite of the elite of the elite of all nuns in the world. Only very wealthy high-stepping young women are allowed into the "convent" schools. Talking really big bucks here, and deep family dynamics. They deserve the fabulous Murphy.

The Madams and the Jesuits have paired up since about 1650. The Jesuits really wanted to get deep into the Court of Louis XIII. The French believed that the heart of the king is itself divine. The Jesuits seized on this and concocted the Devotion to the Sacred HEART of Jesus. The Son of God conveniently revealed his heart to a nun named Saint Margaret Mary. (Think of all the young Catholic women, including my own sister, named Margaret Mary.) The heart looks like a huge strawberry and, in no time at all, portraits of the Sacred Heart are commissioned, made into wall calendars, and hung on walls of Catholic living rooms all over the world. The Madams are in on this from the beginning. They hold the cash until a Jesuit comes around to collect it.

The Madams and the Jesuits have an arrangement to maximize the wealth-gathering potential that comes from working together.

The Madams' school in Seattle is called "Forest Ridge" and is about a half-mile away from Seattle Prep. Murphy goes there every morning to hear confessions and to say Mass.

To give you an idea of the prestige involved, Forest Ridge is the very school that Mary McCarthy attended as a teenager. That was about the time of World War I. Later she became one of America's top writers. She wrote a best seller in the 1960's named, The Group. Her Forest Ridge experiences are in the book, Memories of a Catholic Girlhood. Mary McCarthy is known to take no sass from the big guys.

You should read her book about her Catholic girlhood. It is just excellent. I didn't read it until a few years ago. Why I didn't read it before is the story of these very pages, my story of sexual ignorance. Some older Jesuits at Seattle Prep whispered to us about Mary McCarthy. They say she is Irish-Catholic but is excommunicated by the Catholic Church because she "lost" her virginity to a communist. I wanted to ask these whispering Jesuits if it was Stalin or Lenin.

While the various Jesuits at Seattle Prep are getting up at five a.m., saying prayers, attending mass, receiving communion, and looking forward to breakfast, Fr. Jack Murphy, S.J., of Bald Eagle fame, gets into his Ford Edsel and drives himself up Interlaken Boulevard to the Convent of the Madams of the Sacred Heart. There he hears the confessions of the teenage young women (Forest Ridge is also a boarding school) and the nuns, then he says Mass with utmost pious rectitude, blesses the community, and returns to the Jesuit residence for breakfast.

In the Jesuit residence, breakfast is always in silence. If Murphy is late arriving for breakfast, we chat amiably with one another. It feels good to gossip with your fellow foot soldiers around the breakfast table.

Except when Murphy sneaks up on us all and begins to chew ass for breaking the rule of silence. It is as though he is personally insulted if we talk to each other while he is confessing the Madams. After the ass chewing for not keeping the rule of silence during breakfast, I exit the residence itself. I proceed to the first floor of the school and resume my duty in enforcing silence on the freshmen and sophomores. This is the context in which I become a junior grade bully as well as a hypocrite. Is this the beginning of self-hatred?

CHAPTER 22: LOGICAL POSITIVISM IS AN OCCASION OF SIN. PLUS TWO MORE PEDERASTS.

But I found a way to compensate for the vanity of my Jesuit existence.

Seattle Prep is directly across from the University of Washington. Lake Union lies between. On Sundays I walk over to the University. There is just nothing else to do at Prep except watch television and get into arguments about which program to watch.

The University of Washington, you must remember, is the home in the Northwest of Darwin and the Origin of Species. Therefore, simply walking its campus is an occasion of sin. Best to be careful about these trips. Maybe carry a rosary or some holy cards to ward off any sneaky influence of Darwin.

At first I wear the roman collar while I walk. No one ever gives me funny looks. After a couple of trips I take off the collar and stick it in my coat pocket. Am I searching for something? Perhaps a young woman in a blue dress with an ample bosom?

But I do find the bookstore, and I enter. Ahh, there it is, the section on philosophy. Since I have actually taught philosophy, this is what I am looking for. I want to read books on philosophy.

There is A.J. Ayer's book, Language, Truth, and Logic. I have read about him in Time magazine, and surely he must be a satanist. He is the enfante terrible of Logical Positivism. I read a few pages, and realize that this is very potent stuff, like maybe you've been smoking Pall Malls, and Ayer is hashish.

I put it back on the shelf, and moved down the aisle. Next I found Bertrand Russell's Why I Am Not A Christian. Kahboom! His style is for me, just delicious, elegant and literary. Easy to read.

But I can't buy any of these books, since I have no money. But I have planted the seed in my noggin, just by browsing there. I'll be back the next week.

The next Sunday I begin my usual penniless stroll to the University. The roman collar is in my coat pocket. I'm feeling juiced. I'm halfway across the Montlake Bridge on my way to the bookstore.

Whoah! What's that? On the sidewalk, at my feet is a twenty dollar bill. It's real green, almost as green as I am.

I step on it. No one is in sight. Cars are speeding by. I am afraid to even bend over to pick it up lest a bolt of lightning strike me on the spot.

Reason and common sense soon prevail, and in a flash the bill is in my pocket. I quicken the pace. The twenty dollar bill is an occasion of an occasion of sin. Once it is in my pocket, that is another occasion of sin. And I haven't even got to the bookstore yet.

Obviously, without a shadow of a doubt, God Almighty, hearing the pleas of St. Michael the Archangel, has deigned to reward me for my patience. The twenty is an omen from on high that I have a duty to buy Ayer's and Russell's books. An absolute duty, no less!

I go to the bookstore and buy the books. There is also another book for sale there. It is by Paul Blanchard, entitled, American Freedom and Catholic Power. I can tell just by reading the preface that this is real dynamite. I buy it also. I keep it in my possession but don't read it. I just didn't dare. Since I left the Jesuits, I have read it several times, and it is still helpful to me.

The rest of that year at Prep, between laundry deliveries and classes, my nose is in Russell and Ayer. Russell is my delight, while Ayer is tough going for me, but I stay with him, and in time I begin to groove with him. I am not consciously looking for a replacement to Aquinas. However, Ayer's reasoning and style force me to take him seriously.

Other Jesuits at Prep think I'm in my room smoking cigarettes and listening to the radio. But I'm making a sentence outline of Ayer's book chapter by chapter. I take a paragraph of his and reduce it to one sentence. By God, I will understand this stuff. I emerge from my room only to attend the drunken orgies on Friday afternoons.

About here I want to bring you up to date concerning the pederasty line up at Seattle Prep. The first is Father Dave King, S.J. He is tall and skinny. His head looks like Regis Dinky's bleached skull. He emits not an ounce of affect. He has no friends in the community. He is also a Latin teacher of the 'A' and 'B' classes for the freshmen, and the religion teacher for these same groups. He carries his breviary (a book of Latin prayers which a priest must read from everyday) with him everywhere, even to basketball games. He is the personification of creep. Some of us talk about him.

What is so remarkable about him is that every day when school is out he descends to the locker room and athletic dressing room and mingles with the lads as they undress. This he does every day, all year long, when they leave for practice or for a game. King then returns to his room and corrects papers. Then when practice is over, he rushes back to the locker room until all the lads have left. During these periods in the locker room he displays his breviary like a talisman. "Look, people, see this prayer book? I am a holy man. Give me some slack in the locker room with the young boys." His creepiness is tangible in the community. In my opinion it is not possible to take any satisfaction in being on the Prep faculty with this guy hanging around.

The other pederast is Father James Hess, S.J. He teaches history to sophomores. His students like him since he teaches them nothing and they can dink off all they want. He does not go near the dressing room and I never hear of any complaints from students about him.

But, boy!, does he ever like me. He stands at the community bulletin board as I try to read stuff there, and pats me on the back, then strokes my arm, and tells me how nice-looking I am. He's not King, a creep; but he is definitely a middle-age faggot.

Please realize that if a woman tells me I'm nice-looking, I take (forbidden) pleasure in the compliment. But if a guy says it to me, I don't like it at all. My reaction is: what does he want from me? I try to avoid Hess, but his room is exactly next to mine. If I step out, he is there to greet me, and he tries the arm stroking stuff. He keeps a bottle in his room but closes the door only at night. Sometimes he stands at the doorway sipping from a glass. I can smell the whiskey on him. Often he asks me in for a drink.

Hey, I got burned once before in Father Gene LeGault's room. I don't even consider the offer.

You're thinking: Casey, why don't you tell him to fuck off?

My response is: I don't know how! This goddam vow of obedience has wiped me out altogether. The poison of respecting priests has paralyzed me.

This is how the entire Church operates: All priests are untouchable. After all, they consecrate the host during Mass, the wine becomes the Blood of Christ. His very hands are sacred with the oil of ordination. Leave The Priest Alone! He gets to do anything he wants to.

By now I accept Fathers King and Hess as a normal part of the Jesuit community, just part of the picture. What we have in common is that we are all serving the Kingdom of Christ: Bhah! Why am I not more depressed?

CHAPTER 23: HOPE FOR THE BULLY

In 1962 I had been in the Jesuits for ten years. My question was: Will the heirarchs in the Oregon Province approve me for the study of theology? It is the last phase of Jesuit formation. I thought that the ritual of approval would be a breeze.

The approval was preceded by a visit to the Seattle Prep community by Father Provincial. A scholastic visited with this religious superior during a ritual called "Manifestation of Conscience." During this exercise you were expected to tell everything about your life. My previous visits with the Provincial had always been routine: a quick in-and-out, maybe something trivial was mentioned, such as, "Well, I had missed saying the daily rosary several times."

But in 1962 my final year of teaching as a scholastic, Father Provincial, whose name was Angus MacDonald, S.J. proceeded to really grill me about my deepest intentions. "Do you really want to proceed forward to ordination as a priest?" The grilling went on for some time, as though he wanted me to admit that I am not serious about the religious life. "Are you really sure that this is what you want?"

I begin to think, "This guy doesn't trust me or what I am saying." And if he doesn't trust me, then I'm not going to trust him. Let him figure out for himself what I'm like. I volunteer nothing to him.

It also flashed on me that perhaps Fr. Regis Dinky had forwarded a denunciation of me from our Yakima conflict. Maybe others had managed to put an X behind my name.

MacDonald gave me a personal grilling. It didn't seem formal. The pressure was on me, not on him. I could feel my throat constricting, and my answers to his questions were brief and guttural. Merely in virtue of grilling me he communicates to me that I am not a prime candidate to move forward. I feel this uncertainty from him.

MacDonald is looking in my direction but he does not actually make eye contact. In all, I felt that his approval of me for the study of theology was up in the air.

I left the manifestation of conscience not knowing if I had any reason for hope. For the next couple of months I held my breath as to my fate.

The Catholic Church had always taught that hope, like faith and charity, was a theological virtue not a natural one. But, as in many things, the Church doesn't practice what it teaches. Its practice is to stifle and frustrate hope. Women cannot hope to be ordained priests although it is perfectly possible for a woman to be ordained a priest. Male clergy cannot hope to be married, although it is perfectly possible for this to occur. Their children are declared 'bastards'. And so on for other points of the Church's sexual ignorance. If hope comes only from God, why does the Church work so diligently at suppressing it?

May I say that hope is an aspect of striving. It comes from your own self, on the one hand, and on the other, the objective situation you're in. Without hope, a person will fall into despair, with all the destructive psychological paralysis that condition implies.

This episode with MacDonald took a lot out of my guts. What I have in my guts is confidence and integrity. What I realized then was I had to be very protective of my confidence. Hope for me will not be coming from the Jesuits.

Finally, the school year is over and the Province status report is posted on the bulletin board. This way MacDonald did not have to make eye contact with me. I was assigned to Regis College in Toronto, Canada. I had dared to hope to be sent to Rome. But MacDonald sent only approved "queers" there.

Before I got on the Great Northern's Empire Builder in Seattle, I spent several days giving myself a good-talking-to about how I am beginning a new phase of my life, and by golly, I will change some things about myself. It really bothered me that at Prep I was thought of as a bully. That was the main feature of my character that had to drop out of sight. The bully stuff meant that I was becoming like hierarchs that I despised.

Notice that here I am placing the emphasis for change on myself, the lonely individual in the Jesuit trench. But is that where the pertinent emphasis should be placed? Could it be that it is the Church and the Jesuits that need to change? And not Mike Casey, the solitary swimmer in the sea of fate.

Vatican II would supply an answer.

Of course, I was deluded about all of this. I can never change as long as I am in the Church and the Jesuits. The oil and grease on the gears of the Church is double think. The Church will never change even though it preaches that there are three theological virtues: Faith, hope, and charity. You know how it goes: endless sermons about charity (now called love), and mindless blather about faith (even the greediest pigs on Earth, Mitt Romney and Pat Robertson, call themselves men of faith). But when was the last time you heard a sermon about hope? It's always about how the Church cannot change (e.g., there can never be any women priests, there can never be any gays allowed inside the Church, never any this or that). You know those blood-suckers in Rome really mean this. And so there is never any hope. No hope for gays, no hope for women, no hope for Darwin, no hope for the Caseys.

But in 1962 I thought I could change myself, and so I got on the train for Toronto, still clutching my delusions.

CHAPTER 24: SOLICITATION OF SEX IN THE CONFESSIONAL

When I arrived at Regis College in Toronto, the Second Vatican Council had just begun. The teaching staff knew nothing about it. The courses were divided into Dogmatic Theology, Moral Theology, Canon Law, and the New Testament.

The New Testament was taught by Father Borbely, S.J. He had been the provincial of the Hungarian Province before the Russian Tanks in the 1956 Revolt chased all the Jesuits out of the country. Many of them arrived in Canada. Father Borbely was a small, impish guy with a positive personality and a good sense of humor. Everyone liked him even though he could not speak much English. No one had any idea of what he was saying. He was there to learn English at our expense. He could manage to utter, "...Dah Kinkdah Jesu Christi." In all, his course convinced me that we were not supposed to know or learn anything about the New Testament.

Canon Law was taught by Father MacGuigan, S.J. He was a good-sized man and projected a kindly and jovial attitude about the endless excommunications which the Church could unleash on Catholics who went astray. In his jovial way he still warned us about the Masons (he didn't mean bricklayers!). They could receive Absolution from their heinous crimes (which were never identified) only by a specialist in Canon Law. Absolution was given only after the Mason promised to utterly repudiate the Masonic religion. Also, he was required to cough up names of other Masons.

Also, there were layers upon layers of invalid marriages. All Catholics who entered into matrimony had to have their marriage "blessed" by the Church. May God have mercy on those Catholics who had been divorced and now wanted to marry again. These could be fixed up, but it would cost the wretch tons of money.

Most of this dreck I just tuned out. But my ears perked up when MacGuigan began discussing crimes of the confessional. The main crime here was solicitation. A priest hears a woman's confession, and then asks her to go to bed with him. This is solicitation. I could hardly believe my ears at this. But the next crime in this category, and even worse, was if the priest promised to give the woman Absolution from her sin with the priest. Thus this would be two distinct sins: (1.) The priest solicits sex in the confessional; and then (2.) promises Absolution for her by himself. (Myself, I would add another sin, the abuse of a woman by a priest.)

All this shocked me so much that I just could not believe any of it.

But several years later, after I was ordained a priest, a woman in one of my classes at Seattle University told me of this exact horror. She was driving a drunken Jesuit home from a party. When they got to the Jesuit residence, the Jesuit started to beg her for sex. She said no, and then he began to pull at her clothes. She began to fight him off. Then he said "Oh, come on, I'll give you Absolution afterwards, and then you will not be in the state of mortal sin."

She said that finally she managed to push him out of her car, and drove off.

Now, here's the thing: I knew who this Jesuit was. But where do you think this Jesuit learned this infamous charade? Do you think it could be from his study of Canon Law?

Dogmatic Theology was just ridiculous. It was not even hot air. It was nine months of tepid air. At the end of the year there was a half-hour oral exam conducted in Latin by the very teachers who had supposedly taught you this precious garbage. Many of us mocked this passion play.

The big star at Regis College had been Father Bernard Lonergan, S.J. But he had achieved so much eminence that he was promoted to the Gregorian University in Rome. He had published his master work Insight. It was eight hundred pages of fine print, devoted to synthesizing Aquinas, Immanuel Kant, and Lonergan.

Lonergan had left his lieutenant, Father Fred Crowe, S.J., in charge of Theology at Regis. Sometimes you could understand what Crowe was teaching, but the entire thing never stuck together. Did Christ proceed from the Father and the Holy Ghost, or did the Holy Ghost proceed from the Son, and back to the Father? Who knew? It all sounded like the old barn dance called "Skip To My Lou."

Boogaloo and, Skip to my Lou,

Father, Son, and Holy Ghost too,

Jesus, Mary, and little Joe,

Let's dosey doe,

Doing the Lord's Boogaloo.

What I remember most about Crowe was his habit (defense mechanism, really) of gripping the teacher's podium with one hand and clutching his wrist watch in the other. Actually he lectured to his watch. And so time was on his mind. Your eyes were on that watch for the entire fifty minutes. He was actually communicating to us the eternal question: When will this stuff be over?

In all the classes I sat in the very front row. Occasionally I would raise my hand to ask a question. Crowe would not tolerate questions. He would only say, "No time for questions. I'm cramped for time." Then he would resume lecturing his wristwatch. Since this was the Middle Ages, there never was a class discussion. Several times I tried to corner him after class, but he shot out of the lecture hall like a rocket. I knew he didn't like me, but was he also afraid of me?

But the real pussy in Dogmatic Theology was Father Tibor Horvath, S.J. He was another Hungarian expatriot. A Cuban Jesuit whispered to me that in Cuban slang, Tibor meant piss pot. But the difference between Tibor and Borbely was that Horvath fallaciously believed he was speaking good English. This made the fifty minute lecture even more painful because his pride in his non-command of

English was very irritating. His course was titled, The Catholic Faith. But he could not say "Faith." It always came out, "Zah Faydz." This is an example of Loyola's Black is White doctrine. You think Tibor Horvath is speaking Hungarian but he says he's speaking English. Therefore he's speaking English.

Many of the class leaders went to the Father Superior to complain about Tibor's irritating performance. The Superior told them that he is speaking English, and so it was the class's problem.

Obviously, Father Superior informed Tibor about the classes' displeasure with him. Thus, at the next class Tibor lectured us about our lack of appreciation, why it is true that he is really speaking English.

He stood in front of us, and said, "I really tryink, you guyz. Pleeze, Za Faydze ist hardge class teach." This went on for some minutes. Tibor was choking on his words, breathing hard, and pacing back and forth on the podium, really worked up about this rejection by the class.

Then he turned to me in the front row, "And you, Meestar Kaaze, all time you look so mean. Angry, hah! You look so mean, Meestar Kaaze, all time, so mean."

Then he burst into tears and sobbing. Tibor had succumbed to battle fatigue, and I was his enemy.

CHAPTER 25: FATHER COITUS INTERRUPTUS

From the beginning of time, Moral Theology was the crown jewel of Jesuit power and influence. And the crown sat on the leonine head of Father Ed Sheridan, S.J. He was also the superior (Father Rector) of Regis College.

Father Sheridan struck fear into my heart the very first moment I saw him. This fear did not abate since it was complete from that moment. He still appears in my bad dreams as a menacing figure of scorn. He didn't even have to articulate his contempt of me. It was frozen on his face. He was an ideal Jesuit.

He was known by his nickname: "Butch." Butch was about six-feet three inches tall with the handsome face of a brutal Irishman. He looked like Whitey Bulger, himself a cold professional killer. He was also most articulate. He spoke in complete sentences with no clichés. I don't recall anyone speaking back at him. In his presence everyone was a coward.

And his hands! I'll never forget them: encrusted with thick scaly eczema. As superior he always said the main mass. The guys line up at the communion rail, mouths open as Butch reached into the chalice to lift a wafer and place it on your tongue, the very Body of Christ borne aloft by Butch's fingers of eczema. Once I caught myself looking at his palms to see if there was hair growing there. O.K., so I'm fearful and superstitious.

Moral Theology itself is the moral teachings of the Catholic Church. None of this is from the New Testament. Rather it is a long list of sins and prohibitions drawn from the Old Testament. In fact it is organized in the format of the Ten Commandments. In the hands of celibate clerics the majority of the course was about the sixth commandment.

You recall Big Six, don't you? Yeah, no fucking outside of marriage. Ever! Spoken by the celibate Sheridan.

This took the form of absolute unconditional taboo on "artificial" contraception. Natural contraception was then known as the rhythm method. This did not refer to listening to Muddy Waters or

B.B. King during sexual intercourse. It meant – Ah, shit, who cares what it meant. It was just more clerical authoritarian B.S. to intimidate God's good folk from living their lives as natural human beings.

Butch's crusade for perpetuating sexual ignorance was total war. Hostages are never taken. Human autonomy will be crushed in the rubble.

Take the natural law doctrine about abortion: every abortion is a moral sin. All who participate during an abortion are part of an unspeakable evil: the obstetrician, nurses, and the hospitals. Admitting staff are all equally guilty, maybe even the guys in the parking lot.

Here's a case to illustrate the Church's thinking: A woman is pregnant. But she will die if she carries the fetus to term. But she will live if the fetus is aborted. Aborting the fetus to save the mother's life is using an evil means for a good and just end. Natural law (the Church) stipulates that abortion is murder and can never be allowed, even if it saves the mother's life.

Sometimes life is tragic and complicated. Yet it is not complicated for the Butcher Sheridan. He teaches that in the doctrine of natural law any tragedy is impossible. Natural law is a product of human reason, and tragic choices cannot be allowed to interfere with the workings of reason.

So, the mother dies as a consequence of Church teaching. But the Church and Butch did not kill the woman.

The bare reality is that the woman simply died. Consider this monstrosity of human reason:

The Woman Simply Died.

No choices were made. Nor can they be made. The mother just died, and no moral theologian is responsible for this abomination.

Butch Sheridan did not think up this abomination all by himself. He learned it during his studies in Rome where he wallowed in the Vatican sewer with the other Papal pigs.

And oh say, can I share with you another of my unbridled opinions?

What is the effect of this natural law teaching on young men in seminaries and in Butch's classroom? The above case about the dead mother deepens itself into the noggins of these impressionable male clerics. They are being taught that women are not as valuable as men, and that they do not have any rights over their own bodies. This is the wide-ranging effect of Butch's teaching.

And let me tell you, that when the young clerics at last enter into the real world outside the barren walls of priestly studies, this negative attitude is not easy to shake off. It colors the guy's judgment.

That the Old Testament was the foundation of the Church's teaching on moral theology, let us recall the infamous ONAN, a Jew or an Egyptian in ancient times who "spilled" his seed. The Catholic Church always said that Onan deliberately (with the full consent of the will) pulled his dick out of the woman's vagina, and shot his wad onto the mattress or sheets. O.K., so he didn't want to be liable for child support payments. But, with what it costs nowadays for raising children, who can blame him? The Church term for this is "coitus interruptus."

It has often been said that the Catholic Church is phallic centered; that is, no women priests. I would say, however, that it is seed centered. The phallus is certainly useful for passing on the seed. But the seed is what the Church protects, and the seed can never be wasted.

There is a canon in the laws of the Church concerning conditions for Ordination to the priesthood that states:

The candidate can have his penis amputated, and still be ordained. But if he has his testicles removed, he cannot be ordained.

Well, I at least suspect there is such a canon, even though I can't remember its number.

But here is how the aspiring moral theologian Mike Casey thought of all this (which sin, in fact, he had never heard of before). What if Mr. Onan got very excited, or too excited, before intercourse, and just plain, and shot his wad prematurely? Have you thought of that, Father Butch, huh? Would that be the sin of Onanism?

I considered proposing this objection in class to Father Ed Coitus Interruptus, S.J. But when I got to class, with my brilliant objection in mind, my hands began to tremble, and I felt my throat constrict. Naturally, I was gutless and just sat slumped in my chair seat, defeated again.

Next I need to tell you about the Jesuit mail censorship, Look Magazine, and how Mike Casey was driven nearly to the brink of disbelief in St. Michael's sacerdotal plan for him. These conditions will no doubt seem insignificant to you now. But at the time they were like a knife pressed to my ribs.

In all Jesuit seminaries, there is a mail censor, usually Father Minister (number two after Father Superior). He examines all the mail, looking no doubt for love letters or money. For any recipient who received incriminating objects, Father Minister would call the scholastic in, and demand a suitable justification.

Once I filled in a subscription card for Look Magazine. I had found this on a seat on the Toronto Subway, and dropped it into a mailbox. In time I begin to receive the magazine. I recall that once there were some photos in it of Jackie Kennedy. Wow! Isn't America a great place. The magazine continued to be sent to me for several weeks.

Then, one day in class Butch developed a brief casus conscientiae. Such a casus is an artificial moral dilemma designed to test one's ability to draw precise distinctions aimed at the solution of the dilemma, while sticking to the letter of the law. In secular terms, this is called "petti-fogging," or clever lawyering. As I said, such a casus is always artificial and aimed at tormenting some sad wretch, especially Michael Casey, S.J., an aspirant to Holy Orders in Loyola's Canadian Militia.

Here is Butch's casus. "Suppose some Jesuit scholastic receives in the mail impermissible reading material in his own name, but does not acknowledge this to his Father Superior. Would this be a sin against the scholastic's vow of poverty, or obedience, or both; that is, if this scholastic confessed his impermissible deed, would this be one sin or two? And would the confessor be obliged to give just one penance, or two?"

In all, a real chickenshit problem.

A brief question and answer session ensued, with several desultory comments. No one seemed to care, even though this session was the only one in which the Butcher Sheridan actually opened the floor for comments.

I don't know how many guys in the lecture hall figured out what Father Coitus Interruptus was up to, or what scholastic he had in mind. But some guys there had seen and read Look Magazine in my room.

But the Butcher knew what he was doing. He was instructing and slashing at the same time. These sadists want not only obedience. Really, they need to turn you into a worm so that they can squish you with their size thirteen stompers.

Naturally I was sitting in the front row, a few feet from the Chief STOMPER of the Catholic Church. Positioned there, I was able to read the Butcher's mind. It read: Should Michael Casey load his pockets with bricks, and jump into Lake Ontario? Yeah, should he do this, just for reading Look Magazine without the Butcher's permission? What do you think, guys, now that I have shed the light of Truth on the Sheridan Cesspool?

But it was not Mike Casey who was in the cesspool. Only one guy was there. And that was Butch himself. He had used some cheezie denunciation of me, gathered from the mail censor, to stick a knife in my heart, in order to humiliate me in my own eyes. Of course, Butch did not transgress any canon law. It was a humiliation of me with no obvious "external" harm visible. The Jesuits, like Mafia enforcers, are skilled at issuing silent threats, to the effect, that: "Watch out, sucker, we can get you anytime and anyway we want."

But decency? Come on, Butcher, what about decency?

Butch had thrust a dagger into my heart, full to the hilt. A chill like a large iceberg came over me. This son-of-a-bitch is telling me that I am no good. "All your labor is in vain! Get out, just get out. You don't belong here because you are not like me, the Savage Butch. You are a worm, and I have the power to squish you."

I remember his tone of voice. It was not his usual strident snarl. He was understated. Nor did he look at me. He simply wanted me to know that he alone had the trump card over my feelings as a Jesuit. No gloating or fulminating went with this. It was his personal fatwah upon me. His communication to me was that he was omniscient, and knew each of my secret deeds. Maybe there would be no strangulation followed by burning at the stake. But he could simply cut my balls off.

Why didn't the Butcher just call me into his office, chew my ass, and say, hey Casey, no more Look Magazine?

But that would be efficient and problem-solving. Do sadists seek to solve problems? Of course not. A sadist seeks problems in order to derive the pleasure of inflicting pain and humiliation on the victim. His style is: crush the kid, humiliate him in his own eyes.

When this occurred I was not shook or even jittery. But I was chilled by this sadist, who was also my religious superior, and to whom I was to make a yearly manifestation of conscience.

The Butcher despised me and savaged my soul. Why had he presented this casus conscientiae to the entire class with me in the front row? Obviously, I was his target. There was no necessity for his "presentation" of this artificial casus. There was no point to it all. Was me reading Look Magazine with pictures of Jackie Kennedy at all proportionate to what he communicated to me – that I should consider myself as a worm?

With my well-developed habit of double think I took it all in. How could I defend myself against God's Moral Theologian?

One time I stood at a urinal in the bathroom next to the main classroom. I'm peeing, O.K.? Standing next to me at the other urinal was a certified moral theologian. As I began to finish up my business, he said, "If you shake it once, that's a venial sin. If you shake it more than once, that's a mortal sin." I said to him, "Deo Gratias," and departed from this occasion of sin.

And while we're on the subject, Brothers and Sisters, yes, gathered together in the name of Christ, what do you and I want to know? We want to know how many strangulations and burnings at the stake were necessary to develop the Church's Code of Canon Law?

And how many Whitey Bulgers are still promenading in the sanctuary as Moral Theologians and Canon Lawyers?

But there he is: The Big Guy, setting us all straight. You're hating him, but still focused on him. You wish you could be as rugged as he is, smashing the heretics, and at the same time, just a detestable sadist.

No one can be a sadist unless he or she has an unchallengeable position of superiority over some minion. Casey was the minion, but Sheridan was the sadist, and a coward.

CHAPTER 26: BUTCH SHERIDAN: THE CHAMPION OF PEONAGE

Bear with me while I let you in on more sewage from the Butcher.

When I arrived at Regis College, I was firmly entrenched in the true religion of Christ and Loyola. When I left Regis three and a half years later, I doubted my sanity. It can happen. Of course the Jesuits will say, "Well, it's your fault, Casey. We have Canon Law and moral theology on our side. What have you got besides some stray spermatozoa? Now, please just shut up about the lack of Jesuit humanity and decency."

The disintegration of my spiritual life at Regis seemed to focus on Father Ed Sheridan, S.J. I have already described his vicious doctrines of natural law, and his marauding forays into my own personal life and ethics. Let's call him a jackass for Christ. Maybe he's a captain in the Army of Moloch.

When was it that I decided he was a menace to the People of God? It was when I had to make my first manifestation of conscience to him. In the Jesuit system, the Manifestation of Conscience is the time, once a year, when each scholastic went into the superior's (Father Rector) office, and laid bare all his comings and goings, all his sins, all his likes and dislikes, all his fabrications and personal failings in charity.

You think? Well, it turns out that the manifestation of conscience was the time you prostituted your personal truth-seeking and truth-telling capacities. You're masturbating, and you're gonna tell Sheridan about this? Remember, he's Whitey Bulger. Are you crazy? No one should ever tell the truth to anyone unless it's to his or her personal benefit. And this rules out ever telling the truth to any Jesuit.

The manifestation of conscience is about the same as the Church's Sacrament of Confession, except in the former, your superior, who stands in the place of Christ for you, sits across from you, staring at you, ready to chew your ass, threaten you with extra labors, and mark you out as someone who cannot ever be trusted. And all this is supposed to be for your benefit, and of course, the Jesuit Order itself.

And, while I'm on the subject, remember that the Sacrament of Confession, of which the manifestation of conscience is only a derivative, is a late medieval invention, associated with the Spanish Inquisition and other ethnic cleansing operations of the papacy. It is not a scriptural teaching at all. But, boy oh boy, did it ever catch on, and for many years gave priests enormous power.

But think about this: The confession of sins is no longer practiced in the Church. The Church now has only a general confession of sins. Individuals no longer are required to go into the sweaty box and mumble stuff.

Remember the old days before Vatican II, when a guy went into the confessional box and said, "Bless me father, for I have committed a sin against the sixth commandment?" The priest was required to ask, "with yourself or others?" Then the guy would say, "Well, it was with my girlfriend." Then, the priest would ask, "How many times?" The Church called this the requirement of numero et specie (number and kind).

Confession of sins is the most vile, disgusting, and dehumanizing practice ever invented by the disciples of Satan.

And, the same holds true with the manifestation of conscience.

My turn at manifestation of conscience arrived. I enter the Butcher's office. He says that I may sit. The Butcher sits behind a large desk. Many papers and documents are on it. This shows that he is an important guy.

But wait. In the middle of the desk is a large, rusted double headed axeblade. Ostensibly, this is a paper weight.

Oh, yeah, sure! The Butcher and the axe head! What a combination to show you that your existence under his regime is precarious. In my mind I see pictures of King Henry VIII of England and Ann Boleyn and other wives whom King Henry disposed of with an axe. Am I next?

For twenty minutes he talks and I stutter. Recall the aforementioned Father Regis Dinky, S.J., in Yakima, Washington. Dinky's symbol of power was a metal letter opener, and he wasn't even a superior. But Butch is a big guy, and spoken of, wide and far, as the premier moral theologian in Canada. He's actually interviewed often on Canadian T.V. about artificial contraception (rubbers!).

I have thoughts I want to express to Butch. But he has learned his curled lip snarl from watching Lee J. Cobb or Broderick Crawford on the screen (or have they learned it from him?). I decide that, after all, I have nothing to say. Better for me to just plain leave the Jesuits altogether than to go up against the Lord's own Whitey Bulger, S.J. When I exited, the axe head was still on his desk.

You say, "Well, Casey, aren't you coming down hard, maybe too hard, on Butch? After all wasn't he trying to run Regis College according to the light given to him?"

Listen, the only light given to him was the light of natural law. But the natural law emits no light. Its batteries were dead from the beginning of nature itself. If it did shed light, why was moral theology or canon law invented in the first place? Natural law is empty; it is an empty box. There is nothing in it. Everyone who has reached inside that box has come away empty-handed.

In the stunt he pulled on me concerning the impermissible Look Magazine, Butch showed he had no decency, compassion, fair play, or concern for the interests of others. Therefore, he shed no light. He was a bad example for young Jesuits, who were starting to groove to the teachings of Vatican II.

An example: One day in his class he was expostulating about contracts and a just wage. He did not even mention the minimum

277

wage law. He had only a vague idea of the cost of living increases. No doubt he knew about them but did not mention them.

He spoke of the Church's doctrine of "take it or leave it," that is, peonage. The employer offers a worker two dollars an hour. The worker says, "Hey I need four dollars an hour." The employer says, "Well, take it or leave it. The work is available to you for two dollars. If you don't take it, get moving on down the road. And get off my property."

Of all the chilling things Butch said, this was to me the most chilling. Worse than his teaching of no rubbers, no abortions, and now no wages. Can you grasp his lack of any humanity?

Well, my father and mother both worked for a minimum wage.

Now I ask you, "Am I too hard on Butch?"

Sure, let's have mercy on the prick, but make him work for less than minimum wage, and then see if he can afford even a cheap haircut in a Jesuit barbershop?

Am I bitter? Of course not. I'm merely paying attention, like Madam LaFarge.

CHAPTER 27: THE SOBBING OF THE GUTS

About this time I began to experience physical "break-downs." I would get the shivers and bad colds. My arms and legs and torso trembled inside my cassock. Fevers and sweats. These might last for a couple of days. I managed them with long hot showers. Was this the effect of the on-set of my first Ontario winter?

I was stationed in the Upper Canadian Province (as distinct from the "Lower" French Canadian Province). The Provincial of the Upper was Father Gordon George, S.J. The Jesuit rule is that the Provincial must meet with each Jesuit once a year who resides in his province. His visit at Regis College in 1962 came a few weeks before Xmas. Each scholastic got about ten minutes of his time in his personal office. Mine was about half an hour before the evening litanies, followed by supper.

I came into his room, and he told me to be seated. Then he said, "So, Mr. Casey, how are you adjusting to the Jesuit life here in Canada?"

At the beginning of this interview (in Jesuit terms, it was called a "manifestation of conscience"), I was not intending to tell him anything. I was a Jesuit survivalist and therefore was keeping my conscience to myself (and, more significantly, "from" myself).

After he spoke, I started to say, "Well, I'm doing just fine...fin...fi...fi.., Aghh! Ahgg!..." and I burst into sobbing, my gut heaving up from the floor, gasping for air, sobbing, sobbing. A serious and worthy Jesuit doubled over with the sobbing of the guts. "Ahgg! Ahgg! I am just fin...fi...fi..." More sobbing of the guts.

At that time I had been in the Jesuits for eleven years, and the sobbing of the guts is what I have to show Father Gordon George, the Canadian Provincial. I wished I could just die.

Father George had a box of Kleenex near the desk, and began to hand me some. I had moved him with my sobbing of the guts. He kept handing them to me, but from my eyes, nose, and guts it was all Niagara Falls. He could use a wet mop.

He kept talking, cajoling, saying soothing words. But it took another ten minutes before I got my breath, and paused long enough to tell him what was driving me insane.

Then, I got it out, the unspeakable carbuncle of shame and lies of Mike Casey, S.J., that I had masturbated often and regularly, and that I can't live with this.

Father George, it happened, was the coolest Jesuit I ever met. He got up from his chair and came around to my side, and just so lightly, patted me on the shoulder. He said, "What you told me is good and courageous." Then he sat down at his desk. At last I said, "So, what do I do?"

He said, "I think you're a fighter, and are not afraid of things, perhaps, only yourself." Then he added, "I think you'll be alright, but it will take time and resolve."

He did not say, "I think it will take prayer." For not saying this, I was so grateful; you have no idea of how fed up with prayer I was.

There, in December 1962, someone, an authority figure who wasn't an authority figure, received Michael Casey into the Kingdom of Humanity.

Then he said, "You should just skip going to litanies and supper, go to your room and lie down and rest until you feel better."

In the context of Regis College, Butch Sheridan, and my physical collapse, he was such a wise man. It can happen.

I left his room on the first floor as he went to litanies and supper. My room was on the third floor, but I didn't make it there. Halfway, I quit the climb and sat down on the steps. I was not sobbing or even shaking. I merely sat, numb and stupefied.

After, a few minutes, I began to shake and shiver. I forced myself to return to the first floor, where the community infirmary was. I needed to retire to sick bay. In my delirium, I plain knew this.

In time, the infirmarian, Brother Olney, arrived there, saw what my condition was, and put me into a very warm bed, with heated blankets, gave me a glass of hot water with a small dose of whiskey in it, and a solid, very solid, sleeping pill.

Then I slept until about seven o'clock with Father Butch Sheridan hovering over me, saying Latin stuff, and giving me the consecrated host. Butch said, "Corpus Domini Jesu Christ, etc." I swallowed the host and fell back to sleep. I slept on and off for about four days, with the aid of sleeping pills.

Father George had given me the light to go forward. And I entirely meant to. As he said, I was a fighter, and I didn't know how not to be. But, there was still Butch Sheridan, moral theology and canon law entrenched on the bunker on the hill ahead of me.

CHAPTER 28: OSCAR MENDEZ

A Cuban Jesuit, Oscar Mendez began to assume a role in my life. There were about ten to fifteen Cubans at Regis College. This was the result of Castro's take-over. I wanted to learn Spanish and thought that grooving with Cubans would give me a leg up. But, they all wanted to learn English.

It was Oscar who first cottoned on to me. He had a guitar of his own and offered to help me learn how to play. He played Spanish songs like Malagueña. I was a terrible singer and a klutz at chording. But Oscar stayed with me.

But, at least from him to me, it was much deeper than the guitar. During Xmas vacation (no classes) of 1962 to 1963, he and I would go to my room and talk and smoke, and smoke and talk. The infirmarian Brother Olney, had "advanced" me a half bottle of altar wine. I kept it in my room where Oscar and I would talk, sip, and smoke.

He talked about his dad, who was a prisoner of Castro in the Isle of Pines prison. When he spoke of this he could barely control his emotions. And I could tell that he felt great guilt about leaving Cuba and his family.

Oscar sat in my chair by my desk, and I sat on my bed, semi-propped up by pillows, a cigarette ashtray snuggled on my navel. We were both chain smoking. This, as you are aware, is a sign of mounting tension.

Suddenly, Oscar blurted out to me something awful and disgusting that had happened to him.

"You know, Mike, this guy...he got me in his room, gave me booze. When I was lying on the bed, he started to suck me off. He just suck and suck and suck. No, he no quit. I so drunk. Awful, awful. Very bad stuff. Just suck and suck." Oscar's eyes were like water-filled balloons. He put out his cigarette and lit another.

Me lying on the bed, Oscar across the room. Was my supine position a trigger to an image in his mind?

"You know, Mike Casey, you are the only friend I have here." He's reaching out to me. Although I'm the toughest sexual prude God ever invented, I was moved by his anguish.

So moved in fact that I began to tell him my similar story. I told him about the night in the dark bunkhouse fifteen miles south of my home in Parshall, North Dakota. This happened when I was thirteen years old.

A John Deere farm machinery salesman asked me to go with him to visit some prospective customers near the Fort Berthold Indian Reservation. Anyway, his customers are not at home, and it is dark out. This man, Bill Olson, says to me, "Let's go out to the bunkhouse. Maybe someone is in there."

Only a bed is there. Olson pushed me inside towards the bed, spins me around and I land flat on my back. Olson, a large man, is on top of me in full missionary humping mode. He jams his hairy arm across my mouth. I can hardly breathe. He comes and just lies there, won't get off me.

At last he does and we go outside. It's pitch dark and I have no idea where I am or whose farm this is. Now, it's the first existential question of my thirteen year old life. Shall I get back into the Ford pick-up with him?

I had read in true-crime magazines about rape-and-murder. I didn't know what rape meant. But I knew what murder was. My thought was: first, the guy rapes, then he murders. Is Olson going to murder me? Now, in the dark?

Eventually I crawled into the pick-up with him, and he drove back to the town of Parshall. His parting words were, "Don't ever tell anyone about this!" This miserable cocksucker actually said this! Is there no end to the wretchedness of pederasts!

And, indeed, I never told anyone about this vile act of Bill Olson and his lasting poison.

From 1948 to 1962-3, from Parshall to Toronto, this deed was buried inside my soul, like shrapnel in a G.I., festering but not removable. It is still there, maybe not festering, but certainly not removable. It has set me apart from other people. The question is what if "they" find out about Olson on top of me in the bunkhouse? Unanswerable until Oscar reached out to me with his secret. So, God bless Oscar, wherever he is today.

Oscar's story and my story, an exchange of sexual malfeasance. A true bonding.

When Bill Olson said to me, "Don't tell anyone about this," he made the final assault on Mike Casey. His deed stained so much of what I felt about people, men and women, that there is no way to quantify it. With my sin-conscious mind, if anyone knew of it, I would be destroyed.

When Oscar told me of his episode, I realized that I had reached the end of my silence and hidden despair. I had to understand myself on a deeper level.

Figure 9 Oscar Mendez and Michael, 1965, at Papa's House, Spokane, Washington

Figure 10 The boy that Bill Olson took into The Bunk House, 1948

CHAPTER 29: WHAT I THINK ABOUT HOMOSEXUALITY

After that bonding moment in my room with Players Cigarettes and the bottle of cheap altar wine, Oscar and I became very close. Was this an instance of "Particular Friendship" between us?

Well, of course it was. And I did not like it at all. But at the same time I really liked Oscar. He was a really good guy, and had much to offer me, and other Jesuits.

I can't help it if I am a prude in this respect. But I did struggle with the underlying issue. I spoke to the Spiritual Father of Regis College, Father Dave Aslein, S.J. about it all. Actually, the Spiritual Father, especially during the last formative year of theology, is a more significant priest than Father Rector, Butch Sheridan.

Father Dave wanted only to talk about the Ignatian Discernment of Spirits. He really tried it with me. And, I thought I could follow what he said. But the fluffy saccharine of the Discernment of Spirits stuff evaporated from my mind within minutes after I left his room.

I told him about my encounter with Oscar Mendez. Aslein thought this was good. But my despair at my relentless masturbations and all the homosexual attention I was receiving (Oscar wasn't the only one) was an increasing obstacle to my peace of mind. Oscar's obsession with me only seemed to make my mind more turbulent.

Oscar did not hit on me. For example, remember Father Jim Hess, S.J. at Seattle Prep – patting me on the back and cooing into my ear? Yeah, him. That's what I mean by hitting on me.

Some homosexuals are very witty and cool to talk with (remember Terry Corrigan?). Some were just brilliant guys that knew so much more than I, especially about literature, politics, movies, art. It was and is a pleasure to talk with these guys. Today they would be called 'gay', and thus now socially acceptable. Nowadays, I know many such gays and like their company. But they don't hit on me, and are not creeps. Times change, and the nation's prejudices weaken, bigotry is seen to be ugly. And this is how any problems I might have with homosexuals ceased to exist. Also, now I have much greater understanding of my own character as a recovering reactionary.

Hey, guys, I like women, that's it, and the homosexual element in the Jesuit Order at Regis College made me think I was going batty.

Well, heck folks, I was going batty.

Here are the fears that were pushing me to the brink of batty-hood.

First, there was my adolescent fear of women (any woman). This fear always made me uncomfortable in the presence of women. I just could barely talk to them. I have no firm opinion as to the cause of this fear. But the fear operated in the background of my mind. And was certainly aggravated by the Church's and Loyola's classification of women as inferior to men; at most they were considered only as fit for producing babies. This doctrine was not openly taught from the pulpit on Sundays. But it was the sodden thinking of the Church and the Jesuits. You know what I mean, for sure.

The second fear was that other Jesuits, seeing me and Oscar Mendez together a lot, would classify me as a fruit ("particular friendships"), or at least queer and abnormal. All of us "straight" Jesuits gossiped about such relationships.

This was actually only an occasional fear, at work only in the context of my friendship with Oscar. In time, this fear would pass as I managed to get the Bill Olson-in-the-bunkhouse and the Father LeGault, S.J. episodes out in the open, and aired freely.

Then, there was my fear of what people would think of me if I left the Jesuits. This fear was mostly fear of letting my mother, father, brother, and sisters down altogether. Our family was entirely overdosing on Catholicism. It was just stifling, obsessive, and physically exhausting. The Casey family was tight, courageous against our poverty, but priest-ridden to the point of the label "dysfunctional" family.

I was at the end of my human wits as to how to deal with my dehumanized condition. I could not even imagine that the Jesuits had kidnapped me and enchained me with my own fears. The Spiritual Father, Dave Aslein, kept me going with his counseling about the "Discernment of Spirits." I tried to groove with his help. But I never got the hang of it. How can these legendary Spirits guide me if I could not even engage my own will, for myself, and my own life? If I could ever engage my own will, it would be obvious that I didn't need the Jesuits in order to live my life. Perhaps when I was eighteen years old, the Jesuits filled some need of mine. But that was then, a decade ago. And this is now.

"Now" means that I had to work everything out for myself, and on my own. Guilt, lies, self-deception, and denunciations had struck deep roots in me. I'm a fighter and a stubborn Mickey, but dammit, for the next several years it was two steps forward and one and a half steps backwards.

CHAPTER 30: LET SMOKEY JOE INTO HEAVEN

The Vatican II Council convened in Rome in 1962, the very year I began the study of theology. It closed in 1965 – the year I was ordained to the priesthood. At the time it seemed to me that the deliberations in Rome mirrored my own personal turbulence in Regis College.

What I have learned since I left the Jesuits was that there was a deep background which brought the Council into existence. Information about this background could only be surmised at the time. But now you can read about it.

The overt purpose of the Council was reform. It was referred to as aggiornamento (an updating, or "for today's world"). About this, all agree.

I'll begin with the person of John XXIII (Angelo Roncalli). In fact, I'll refer to him hence fore as "Roncalli".

Roncalli was the agent of a far-reaching papal Vatical policy. This was the change-over from Pius XII's anti-Communist crusade against Moscow to a pro-Moscow opening to the Eastern "Bloc". Very serious business going on here. As evidence, recall those photos in the main press outlets of Khrushchev's daughter and son-in-law visiting Rome. They had an audience with Roncalli. Everyone was smiling. The Vatican also published a personal note of congratulations to Roncalli from Nikita Khrushchev himself.

The rationale for all of this was the eventual re-unification of the Roman Church with the Russian Orthodox Church. If this transpired, it would be a momentous enhancement of the Vatican Power. It would also be a big winner for Europe itself, which, since World War II, was in thrall to the United States and NATO. This far-reaching scheme was the real or covert purpose of the Council. And rest assured that this policy came from the very highest ruling body that has no name, passes no laws, but decides the fate of all.

So, how did Roncalli get into the center of things?

The answer to that question lies in the persons of Charles de Gaulle and the top French Cardinal in Rome, Eugene Tisserant.

The French side of the story began when de Gaulle recaptured Paris from the Germans in 1944. The Archbishop of Paris, Cardinal Suhard, had been a Nazi collaborator. Therefore the Catholic Church in France is in trouble with de Gaulle.

During World War II, the French Communists owing to their then anti-Nazi stance had become very powerful, and could put the entire country in its grip. Hence, de Gaulle needed someone to grease the diplomatic wheels between the Communists and the Catholics. What de Gaulle is seeking is national unity.

Meanwhile, Cardinal Tisserant is the top Frenchman in Pius XII's Vatican. He is an ardent French Nationalist and understands the situation.

Tisserant knows of Roncalli who had been a Vatican diplomat in Bulgaria during World War II. There he had proven himself kosher by forging hundreds of "Catholic" passports for a very large group of Bulgarian Jews so that they could immigrate to Palestine instead of riding the boxcars to Auschwitz. And Roncalli carried this off. Not your typical Vatican bureaucrat. Just a hell-of-a-guy!

When the situation in Paris between de Gaulle and the Church threatened to blow up, Tisserant sent Roncalli to Paris in the fall of 1944.

Again Roncalli works his charm. He mends the breach between the French Church and the French Communists. De Gaulle is placated. National unity prevails.

It was a long wait from Roncalli's time in Paris to October 1958 (oh, happy day) when Pius XII croaked. Tisserant hovered near the doorway of the papal apartment. He hears the final croak, bursts into the room, orders Pius XII's girlfriend, Sister Pascalina Lehnert (La Popessa) out of the entire Vatican City. She was never seen there again.

Tisserant then arranges for the papal election, makes himself the official counter of the ballots, and bingo! Habemus Papam: it's Angelo Roncalli! Will miracles never cease?

Roncalli begins to open Vatican windows. The air inside is stuffy, isn't it? And speaking of open windows, just how will Protestants and Communists get into the Church?

Hey, brothers and sisters, isn't the Church for all people? Not just the Vatican Shmendricks?

Ever since Roncalli died in 1963 from an overdose of Vatican Arsenic, Catholic liberals have praised Vatican II for changing the Mass into the vernacular, and turned the altar around to face the congregation. I call this the "window dressing" approach to Church reform. So, who cares if you now say "Holy Spirit" instead of "Holy Ghost"? I certainly have lost interest. Besides, I have always loved ghosts, and will groove anytime with a ghost in place of a Catholic liberal.

My point is that actual Vatican policy was to make the Catholic Church the unifying presence in Europe, including Russia. So, just forget about the Mass in the vernacular, and the altar facing the people. That's just for the liberals who get their information from T.V. Remember how they watched the Polish Pope celebrate Mass in Yankee Stadium and applauded. Puppetry mixed with mummery.

As the Council moved along, elements of doctrine emerged.

One of these was a courtesy call to the Jews. The Council removed the petition in the litanies, Ad perfideos Judaeos ("for the faithless Jews"). So, there went two thousand years of denunciations and burnings at the stake. It was rumored that when the petition was removed, Pius XII (Pope Pig) rolled over in his grave, muttering "Goddam Jews."

One of the main questions for the Vatican Council was the role of the Scriptures in the Church.

The idea was emerging that the scriptures were the life of the Church. Instead, in previous centuries the scriptures were only handy rhetorical quotes to shore up Butch's moral theology; for example, "Thou art Peter and upon this rock I will build my Church." This secured papal supremacy, itself a spurious doctrine invented about a thousand years after the time of Christ.

At the time of the Council most of us were impressed with the new emphasis on the Scriptures. In conjunction with the Mass in the vernacular and the altar facing the congregation, we thought we had something to say.

But you know, what can anyone say about the wedding at Capharnaum when Jesus changed water into wine, or when he turned a piece of bread and a few cans of sardines into a massive banquet to feed hundreds? What kind of enthusiasm can a guy generate about some dopey miracle? Do we need a Council to legitimize magical thinking? This is the twentieth century, for crying out loud! No one, except some imbeciles in the Tea Party, believes in miracles anymore. And if they do what do they need doctors for? If I stayed in the Jesuits I would be indistinguishable from Oral Roberts and his illegitimate son Jerry Fartwell.

The Scriptures are even more boring than the philosophy of Aquinas. During Mass now, you hear about the "Lord is my Shepherd." But really, have you ever personally seen a shepherd? In the Twentieth century?

The Council also decreed that the Church was nothing else but The People of God. Was this rhetoric only, or did the guys in Rome really mean it? Myself, I found hope and relief in the teaching. It sounds to my ears like Luther's The Priesthood of All The Believers.

The Church as The People of God also worked to diminish the difference between the hierarchy and the men, women, and children who pay the bills. Very few people got their religion or faith from the clergy. Most people get their religion from their families.

Also the Church had always taught that there are no dogs in heaven. The reason was that no dog had an immortal soul – right out of Aristotle and Aquinas; it had only a dog soul: you could not doubt this. After The People of God decree there could be entire families in heaven; but would the family dog be there as well? Family dogs are integral to families. Are you gonna leave the dog to the likes of Butch Sheridan, the Vatican dog catcher?

Nah! My dog Smokey, whom I inherited from my daughter Dawn, has been dead now for ten years. Smokey departed this veil of tears for the Spirit World; and I will be with him myself in a few years.

The no-dogs-in-heaven b.s. forced me into a quandary. Here's the scene: Pope Pius XII dies and now is heaven. Mike Casey also dies and stands at the reception desk at the gates of heaven. He fills out the usual information forms: age, place of birth, ever had diabetes, syphilis, etc.? Ever been a member of the Communist Party?

Then, Casey asks: "Where's Smokey Joe?"

Mr. Important says, "No dogs allowed in heaven. Hence, Smokey Joe is not here."

Casey blinks. But not for long.

"Mass murderer Pacelli is here but not Smokey Joe? Huh? Go fuck yourself, Mr. Very Important. Take your heaven and shove it up your ass. Count me out!"

Mr. Important tries to reason with Casey: "There can be no deals with God, since God is the ruler of heaven and earth."

Casey is a fighter, and is not moved by these edicts: "It's me and Smokey Joe inside, or Pacelli and Jehovah outside. You dig?"

Mr. Very Important says: "If you demand Smokey Joe in heaven (which can never be), well, you will not be ordained a priest. It's that simple!"

Casey shoots back: "Why don't you do the obvious, and ordain both me and Smokey Joe? Don't dogs need priests? Aren't dogs also children of God?"

The Council changed the liturgy into the vernacular and switched the altar to face the actual People of God. But it didn't go far enough since it retained the priesthood, the bishopricks, and the papal pricks.

Figure 11 Smokey Joe

All the problems in the Catholic Church are caused by the hierarchy and their clerics. If you want Church reform, the thing to do is to get rid of the hierarchy. At least, try the People of God. The People of God couldn't do worse than the clerical goons who have run the Church into the ground for the last two thousand years.

Also during Vatican II there was extensive discussion of the overriding question of the relationship of the Pope himself to all of the bishops worldwide. A word was invented to gloss over these contradictions, and that word was "collegiality". This was another empty box placed in front of the People of God and their bishops. "Collegiality" seems to mean "you guys meet with the Pope, and then his Flunkies will tell you what to do."

Actually, the relationship of the Pope to all the bishops had been decreed as a fundamental doctrine back in 1418 A.D. at the Council of Constance. There had been scads of popes at that time, from Rome to Avignon, and all of them claimed to be thee pope. A few courageous leaders told everyone to meet at Lake Constance, on the north side of the Swiss Alps. The Holy Roman Emperor showed up and hushed up all contenders except a dude from the Colonna family. This family had previously supplied the papacy with several Popes. Mr. Colonna took the name of Martin V. Is it necessary to mention that the Colonna family was the wealthiest of the bunch? It sure helps, doesn't it?

The Council of Constance decreed that a General Council (itself, for example), representing the Catholic Church, possessed its authority from Christ. And all men of every rank and condition, including the pope himself, must obey it in matters of faith.

All Catholic theologians know of this doctrine. And all ignore it as they chant, "The Pope alone is infallible."

Brothers and Sisters, it is simply not possible to reform the Church. John XXIII (Roncalli) gave it his best try. And as a result the Vatican Flunkies poisoned him. So, I'm telling you, just up and leave. Don't even say good-bye. Just get out.

Meanwhile, back at Regis College, we all chewed on these issues. The faculty was completely silent on the Council. They folded their hands and said their breviary. Monkeys in a zoo. But many of us scholastics debated the Church's Teaching on birth control. There were other issues, but birth control (no rubbers) was the most divisive. But we were mainly blind about it since we were ignorant celibates.

Most of us resented the "no rubbers" doctrine because we were the ones who had to preach this reactionary ignorance to the folk in the pews.

Then, Montini (Pope Paul VI) took the birth control issue out of the Council's deliberations, and said that he would establish a commission to study it. In other words, he, not the Council, would hold it to his own infallible judgment.

Like the Kennedy Assassination, every Catholic knows where he or she was in July 1968 when Montini, the Fink, decreed in Humanae Vitae that indeed using a rubber was a deadly mortal sin.

I myself was sitting in the Jesuit coffee club room at Seattle University when the final announcement was made. I had been ordained for three years, and had heard many confessions. At that moment, I just knew that Mike Casey, S.J., and the Church were no longer as one. I just knew it was over. And in a few months, I was gone.

CHAPTER 31: MY PHILOSPHICAL DEVELOPMENT

Remember what I told you about the decree of Father General, John Baptiste Jansens, S.J., that each Jesuit scholastic had to develop an academic specialty so that he might fit into the modern secular world? Yeah, remember when the Dean of Studies of the Oregon Province, Fr. William the Prick Weller, S.J. assigned me to the academic specialty of Latin. Modern world indeed.

Well, in 1963 I was still carrying that fatwah.

However, Fr. Cliff Kossel and Father John (pederast) Leary had secreted me into the teaching of philosophy. But my academic status was still undetermined. By now Weller was dead, like Latin.

So, what do I do?

Exactly. I take matters into my own hands and enroll for summer school at Georgetown University for a course taught by Rudolf Allers, entitled, "The Irrational in Man."

Imagine the irony of me going all the way to Washington, D.C., and Georgetown, to take a course, The Irrational in Man, when all I had to do to master the topic of the irrational in man was to interview the savage sadists on the Regis faculty. Plenty of material there.

Thus, with Father Provincial's approval, it's off to Georgetown for the summer of 1963.

Professor Rudolf Allers had been a disciple and student of Martin Hermann Heidi Humdinger back in Germany in the early 1930s. The Nazi stench hung all over Martin, and Allers sniffed it, and got out of Germany fast. He landed at Georgetown, teaching a sort of "Catholic" version of phenomenology. (Remember that Heidegger had briefly been in the Jesuits before World War I, and was dismissed for wetting the bed. But I digress.)

I went to every seminar meeting, wrote down everything Allers said, read Ernst Cassirer's book, The Philosophy of Symbolic Forms, but just couldn't get the hang of phenomenology. I went to the final exam, read the questions, and tried to fake an answer. Then I pocketed my pen and walked out.

Since I didn't actually hand in the final exam, I was given an incomplete in the course, and this seemed to summarize my summer at Jesuit and Catholic Georgetown.

However, I did keep my philosophical development going by reading authors I was always curious about; e.g. Bergson, Gilbert Ryle and his Concept of Mind. I was confused but not lost. Then, one day in a book store near Georgetown, I found and bought a book titled The Classics of Analytic Philosophy by Ackerman. This book was my philosophic source for the next five or six years, until I was assigned to teach philosophy at Seattle University in 1967.

I never gave Aquinas another thought.

The analytic approach to philosophy became my main direction in teaching philosophy for the next thirty years.

CHAPTER 32: BOURBON, PRIME RIB, AND HYPOCRISY AT GEORGETOWN

That summer in Georgetown in 1963 was illuminating to me in other ways. First, there was the racial turmoil. My first morning there, I and other scholastics went to the funeral of Medgar Evers, who had been murdered a few weeks earlier. The event began at the Lincoln Memorial and slowly proceeded to Arlington Cemetery (Evers had been in the military during World War II, and was eligible for burial there). At the actual burial an honor guard of soldiers fired a five round rifle salute as the coffin was lowered. It was a deep and moving experience as to what a great country America is. You could feel the presence of Lincoln, and the Civil Rights Movement, and hear the sobs of the Medgar Evers family as their daddy went into the ground.

I rode a bus back to Georgetown, and wondered about all this.

About a week later I was walking and sightseeing near downtown Washington, D.C. I spied an array of "Young Republicans for Goldwater." They held placards and signs on sticks. There was much stars-and-stripes about the group. The young people wore sport coats made of red, white, and blue cloth. And the young men wore Yankee Doodle hats (you know, white straw, flat tops, and, again, red, white, and blue ribbons on the hats). They were all white kids (this was in 1963). They were proud and peppy. They stomped their feet and cheered. The contrast with the Medgar Evers funeral could not have been greater.

The young Jesuit scholastics there that summer seemed to be very much in favor of integration, certainly no outright racist talk. But over at the Georgetown Faculty Residence the attitude was different. It was not overt racist talk but you could feel the resentment. These guys did not like how things were going, integration-wise. Mainly, the older priests did not talk about the Civil Rights Movement. Just silence, and trivial questions about how theology in Canada was doing.

But their booze (lots of it) and the prime rib was very good. I liked that part, but not their companionship. Just not my kind of people.

In fact, the conspicuous display and consumption of luxury at Georgetown began to irritate me. It seemed that most of the older Jesuits all were connected to important people in the government, and were adept at name dropping. Sometimes I was invited on their jaunts over to, say, Arlington, Virginia. Parties or soirees were held, and African Americans would serve us supper, and clear the tables. I had never experienced this division of society before.

Indeed, I ate the food, drank the booze, and listened to the important talk. Again, these people were not my kind of people. I realized that I was a poverty prude and a poverty hypocrite. Yet it was these experiences that made me realize that there really was no chance for Vatican II's doctrine that the Church just is The People of God.

I didn't fit in.

If I stayed at Georgetown much longer, I felt that I would become a full hypocrite as a result of Georgetown's visible wealth.

Also, it's the summer of Martin Luther King's "I Have A Dream" speech, and the historic March on Washington. All summer long people are talking about this event. Jesuit scholastics are planning for it. I know how it will go: attend the rally, shout and cheer, and return to the air-conditioned dormitory for bourbon and prime rib.

I weigh all this in my heart.

Social Activism is fine. When the cheering and clapping of hands and the stamping of feet is finished, however, folk go to parties and discuss how they witnessed history. But no one organizes the next day for the revolution. You know what, folks? I am not a social activist. I am a proletariat, and my mother and father and brother worked for minimum wage as I myself had. They can't afford to go to the big rally. For my own self-respect, I can't either.

I, the poverty prude, will split from Our Nation's Capital and Georgetown's conspicuous consumption of prime rib and glasses of bourbon. I will turn my back on the wealth of Jesuit hypocrisy and head north back to Toronto on a Greyhound with the People of God. I will make this trip on the Greyhound, goddamit, back to the land of ice, rocks, Sheridan, and the malarial insanity of moral theology.

CHAPTER 33: ON THE GREYHOUND WITH THE PEOPLE OF GOD

That summer my sister Patty and her husband Eugene Buckmaster, and their young children visited me at Georgetown. Eugene was stationed in the U.S. Air Force just over the hill in Knoxville, Tennessee. My family is unwittingly reaching out to me, or am I reaching out to my family in hopes of experiencing The People of God?

Whatever, Georgetown and the Jesuits do not recognize their existence. They stay at a motel outside Arlington, even though there are many empty rooms at Georgetown. I'm thinking what have the Jesuits ever done for me or my family. The Jesuits will give eloquent sermons and write books about The People of God. But it's just talk, and after the sermon is over, it's back to the bourbon and prime rib.

I begin to think that the Jesuits are merely a mutual anus sniffing society. Do I want to hang around? My motto is: if you've sniffed one anus, well, you've sniffed them all.

Deep resentment boils inside my guts. I pack my suitcase and hop on the D.C. Metro, ride it to the Greyhound Bus Depot. The racist Georgetown Jesuits and the Big Ass March on Washington do not interest me. I'll be on the road again, on the Greyhound back to Toronto. I'll show the world that I'm an ordinary American and ride the Greyhound with Ordinary Americans, the People of God.

GO GREYHOUND! GO VOW OF POVERTY!

The bus will be leaving at nine p.m., and I have about five minutes to buy a ticket to Toronto and drag my suitcase packed with the Classics of Analytic Philosophy, six small cans of V-8 Juice, and several pickles wrapped in wax paper. I had lifted these from the Jesuit cafeteria. This was my dietary atonement for all the bourbon and prime rib I had guzzled and chewed on at Georgetown.

It's about nine o' clock and I hurried to the waiting Greyhound. The driver stands at the door and says, "Hurry, Father. We're leaving right now. There's just one seat left for you."

He pointed to a seat just one row back on the inside row. I took one step toward it.

I also took a look up the length of the bus. Sixty pair of eyeballs sized up this Mickey with a roman collar and a black woolen clerical suit. Huh? They all think: what's he doing here? These eyeballs signaled to me that I didn't belong on the bus.

Are you aware that priests never ride the Greyhound? The eyeballs all said get back to your limousine. How dare you travel with the common people of God! How can we look up to you as a representative of the Holy Father in Rome if you, just like the Word Himself, are made Flesh and dwell among us? Priests do not travel on the Greyhound. Hey, Father, get over it. We are all Catholics, rosary, Mass, and confession of the sins. But we do not trust you. Please, Father, do not embarrass us with your clerical status. You have lots of money. What are you doing on this bus? This makes you a phoney. Maybe you are showing us that you are one of us, when indeed you are not.

I then looked at the seat designated for me. Only one person sat there. A double seat, one occupant, and no room left for the other hypothetical occupant, Michael Casey, S.J., who is on the bus in the first place because he is fed up with the wealth of Georgetown University and the Jesuits who own it.

I'm standing and the bus is inching forward out of the depot. The driver said, "No standing in the aisle, Father, while the bus is in motion." I took the plunge and squeezed my right bun and leg into the remaining space.

The woman in the seat weighed at least 300 to 350 pounds. She wore a sleeveless blouse. Massive slabs of overindulgence in supermarket pizza and doughnuts careened to her left and to her right. The bus is hot, and the city is muggy. Was there a chapter in Loyola's Spiritual Exercises that discussed this type of situation?

Meanwhile the sixty pair of eyeballs are watching me. How will Father Mickey, S.J. handle the flab?

Is there more to riding with the People of God than I originally thought?

I got my left bun in to the seat by forcing my right leg hard against the very fattest of God's People, but at the cost of dangling my left leg over the armrest and let it stick out into the aisle. Much priestly decorum is on display.

Soon, the bus is on the freeway headed north.

From my right came the question: "Say, Father, do you know Father Polasky? He's our priest in Pittsburg. We really like him. He's not stuck up at all!"

"No. I don't know him. I've never been to Pittsburg."

"He's at the Shrine of Our Lady of Fatima there. He leads the rosary. And during Lent he says the Stations of the Cross."

I should have stayed in Washington, D.C., for the Martin Luther King speech. Instead I get Father Polasky.

"Father Polasky, hey, don't you know him?"

Then, she makes to dive into her massive handbag. Rosaries and a fist full of holy cards emerge from the handbag.

She makes this move and her upper arms slap into my shoulder and face. More stuff comes out of the bag. Does she have pizza or Kielbasa sausage in there? I might be interested.

"Here, Father, you wanna stick ah chooun gum?

I pass on the gum. The bus rolls on into the night headed north.

One seat ahead of me but across the aisle sat a man and a woman. When I got on the bus, I noticed that they were smooching. In 1963, before Woodstock, people who smooched in public were considered cheap. I began to be aware of them again as a pair of blubbery upper arms slapped against me. The woman across the aisle would occasionally withdraw from the public carnal embraces, turn her head around and give me a long look.

She also smiled at me. Was I the next seat mate? No thanks, Hon, I'll stick to the disciple of Father Polasky and her chooun gum.

Is this what it's like for a Jesuit in a black woolen suit and a roman collar to be traveling with the People of God on the Greyhound Bus? Anyway, Father Master would be proud of me. But I never heard of any other Jesuits traveling on a bus. Am I just delusional?

Of course I was. The vow of poverty was merely a formal operation. The Jesuits are wealthy, and God's people know this. But Jesuits never travel on the Greyhound. Not even Father Master rode it. He took the train or had another Jesuit drive him in the Buick.

About midnight the bus rolled into Harrisburg, Pennsylvania. Mr. Smoocher across the aisle got off. Miss Cuddles was alone in the seat. She kept looking at me. Finally, as the bus trip resumed, she announced, "There's room for you, Father, over here. Aren't you kinda squeezed where you are?"

I, the Jesuit hypocrite, ignored her.

The bus I'm on is an Express; that is, it doesn't stop at small towns. It moves from Harrisburg, PA north to Binghamton, NY.

At Binghamton, we get a half-hour break to pee and drink a soda. I drink a V-8 Juice and eat some pickles. The disciple of Father Polasky transfers to elsewhere. Cuddles sits alone in her seat. Father Mike stands in the aisle, as do other newcomers. Now, the bus is a "local"; that is, it stops every ten or fifteen minutes to let folk from smalltown America in New York State get on, and off. We're in the Finger Lakes district of New York State. Much getting on and off.

Around three p.m. the bus arrives at Syracuse. I pop open a V-8 Juice, and chew a pickle. I've ridden with the People of God for eighteen hours. Sweat rash erupts near my roman collar.

I slouch in a chair in the Syracuse Bus Depot, hoping to fall asleep and miss my connection to Rochester and to Buffalo. A beggar taps me on the shoulder, and says, "Father, can you help me? I need a dollar."

In my wallet there is no dollar bill. I give him a five. He moves on. An older woman on a bench, gets up and stands in front of me.

"Hey, we give that money to the Church for the support of the clergy and the schools. Why do you hand it out to a bum? What's wrong with you?"

She is right. I am an ignorant innocent. The Church is money and nothing but money. "St. Michael, how can I get out of this business of holiness, pseudo-charity, and money religion?"

The bus leaves Syracuse at about four p.m. Then, it's on to Rochester. I sit with a guy who wears a light tan suit. He is not dismayed by the roman collar and the black wool suit that is boiling me alive.

We speak. He's on the bus and bound for Cleveland, Ohio. He sells aluminum siding. He says he was out of work much of last year, but now has it together again. He has no confessional secrets and no chooun gum to dump on me. He's a good guy, about my age with a wife and two kids in Cleveland. We talk about stuff, how he's happy with his job and how things are going good for him. We groove. God Bless him for not asking me about where I'm going, or what kind of shithead I am.

I'm with the People of God and an aluminum siding salesman. These I can identify with.

It's like I'm back in Spokane with Papa, Mama, and Dominic, and Margaret.

I'm the only Jesuit I ever heard of who rode the Greyhound with an aluminum siding salesman. Why must I go back to Regis College and the infinite distinctions of Butch's doctrine about Onanism?

At Buffalo I begin the transfer to a bus to Toronto. Cuddles now stands with her family on the tarmac. I wish her well. I believe that she is a good person. It was a grueling trip for her and the Mickey wearing the collar and the black suit. She departs, and, at 10 p.m. I climb on the bus for Toronto.

When we get to Toronto, it's one a.m. Twenty-eight hours for the vow of poverty, and you know what? No one gives a shit about my pilgrimage with the Cross of Christ's Poverty nailed to my back. Not only that, from the bus depot in Toronto, it's another two hours on the subway and late night city bus to Regis College.

From the bus stop in Willowdale to the front door of Regis College, it's another mile walk. I'm packing a suitcase of heavy philosophy books. I mean pounds, not content.

The front door is locked, and I start pounding on it. Eventually a lay brother named Ken appears and gazes through the window of the front door. Then he disappears, and I keep pounding. Twenty-eight hours of pilgrimage and my eyes are piss-holes in a snow bank. Why don't I just say, "Fuck it!" and go back to the Greyhound?

Then there are voices from inside. They are not soothing sounds. Then a large man appears. He wears a bathrobe. It is Butch Sheridan. He shouts through the locked door: "Who are you? And what do you want?"

CHAPTER 34: THE INQUISITION OF FATHER BRIAN TIFFIN, S.J.

You all think, don't you, that the Spanish Inquisition is long gone, an artifact of medieval moral theology, vanished no doubt like the Black Plague.

Well, it did not vanish. I myself witnessed an actual inquisition at Regis College in Willowdale, Ontario in March 1965. It was the ugliest event I ever witnessed in the seventeen years I was in the Order.

The Inquisition in question was occasioned by the emerging debate within the Church between Butch Sheridan's Moral Theology and Elliot MacGuigan's Canon Law, on the one hand, and on the other, the daring and simplifying teaching of some theologians (mostly European) that "Love is the Answer." This was a conflict between rules, laws, and punishments (excommunication) approach to sinners, and the reaching-out and embrace of all of God's People into the saving mercy of Christ, our Savior. In fact, even if you used a phrase such as "the saving mercy of Christ" you might be put under the cloud of heresy. It was just too Protestant.

The problem with Father Ed is that no human being had ever loved this man for himself. His array of mental and physical talents made him immune to love, of any kind.

Ed had soldiered on in a loveless Irish Catholic and Jesuit world of corporal punishment with the flagellatio and the cras catenellae of the self-inflicted punishment.

Does this reference to self-punishment by physical torture remind you of another Irish Mickey who followed the same trail of blood and tears? Yeah! Exactly! The lost and nearly demented Mike Casey, S.J. himself. Except: my Mother loved me.

I was terrified of Butch and MacGuigan. They could, and would, squelch my hopes of being ordained a priest in the Jesuit Order. They really would do that if they thought that I lined up with the main doctrines of Vatican II, or at least, its spirit that the People of God is the Actual Church. Not only if I lined up in favor of Vatican II, but, especially if I proclaimed favorable words about it.

Here's how the Inquisition of Father Brian Tiffen, S.J. came about.

One day, in the middle of Vatican Two, I was riding the subway from downtown Toronto back to Regis College. Directly across from me was a very strange looking creature. He had the face of a bulldog. I couldn't be exactly sure if he was even human. He wore a funny get-up, as though it were from the fifteenth century, maybe old curtains thrown over his shoulders. And he was ugly beyond description. He held a heavy bag in one hand.

Out of the top of the bag were sticking some small pieces of wood, like you might use to light a fire. In his other hand he held a book with an ancient leather cover. He clutched it to his chest.

He seemed to have been transported across space and time. Just what is he doing in Toronto?

Then, it just flashed on me that this is Tomas Torquemada, the Chief Inquisitor of the Spanish Inquisition. I'm not making this up. To those who believe in miracles, all things are possible. Also, since I'm Irish, I have an uncanny power of intuition.

Then I got up my nerve, and said, "My name is Mike Casey, S.J. I am from the Oregon Province. I was born during the Great

Depression in 1934 in North Dakota. And I was raped in a bunkhouse by Bill Olson.

"I would like to talk to you, in order to understand why you are in Toronto." I didn't bring up the subject of the 2000 Jewish conversos he burned at the stake during his stewardship of the Spanish Inquisition.

I figured if I mentioned the Great Depression, and North Dakota, he might consider that I am on his level of depravity.

He responded well to my subtle and gentle approach. "I'm here on business. A minor Inquisition will be held at Regis College. You ever heard of the place?"

I catch my breath. "Well, yeah! I sure have. Butch Sheridan is the Jesuit Superior there and teaches moral theology. He is very keen on denouncing Onanism, and also denouncing scholastics who have Look Magazine sent to them without Butch's permission."

Torquemada beams and snickers. "Butch is my man in Regis. I have plans to promote him to Holy Office, just as soon as my successor, Cardinal Ottaviani, feeds the arsenic to Pope John XXIII. Then he sneered, "You know, don't you, that Roncalli is a Communist?"

Then he added, "Say, sonny boy, I invented moral theology. Before me, it didn't exist. I myself made the Pope infallible. I inserted the petition "Ad perfideos Judeos" into the litanies. Also, no divorce, no rubbers, no women priests, no sweat equity for janitors and hot lunch cooks. And best of all, no fucking outside of marriage, and no orgasms for women. After I finish burning all the Jews, I'm gonna burn all homosexuals, both male and female. Maybe, I'll turn this project over to the Mormons."

Then I asked him about Bill Olson, the guy who raped me in the bunkhouse. "Are you gonna burn that son-of-a-bitch, too?"

He said, "Hey, watch your language around me. I'm a priest, and I demand some respect. Besides, Bill Olson was not a homosexual. He was married and was merely a rapist. So don't get carried away with burning at the stake for rapists. You have to keep things in proportion."

Whooh! Very heavy information is being passed to me on the subway. Can I handle it?

So, I thought that I would change the subject for a bit.

"And how about Father Elliott MacGuigan, our canon law teacher? He taught us about solicitation of sex in the confessional. Does that actually take place?"

Torquemada pursed his lips, and then said, "Don't worry about it. Most women are hysterical anyway. You just can't believe them. Besides, MacGuigan is himself the chief of Titty-squeezers in Toronto. He gets a pass."

We came to the end of the subway line, and switched to the bus which would take us to Willowdale, and Regis College.

Torquemada kept talking. "Say, have you ever read Father Haring's book, The Law of Christ? I hope you haven't. He cannot be trusted. He thinks love is the answer. Just pathetic. And believe me, sonny boy Casey, I'm gonna crush him. And I'll do it in the name of orthodoxy and papal supremacy. I've got Butch on the job. This sack of wood I'm carrying is the kindling for the bonfire we'll light under Haring's feet."

He continued. "Haring's been in Rome since 1950 teaching the crap that the Church must get rid of moral theology, those hundreds of legalisms based on the Old Testament. Perfideos Judeos! Haring's got the ear of Roncalli. What's love got to do with it, huh?"

The bus had stopped at the entrance to Regis College, and we got off and started walking to the front entrance. My heart had shriveled at the misery of his words.

As we approached the front door, Torquemada's voice got weaker and seemed to trail off. He was walking on my right. I looked towards him. But I couldn't see him. Rats! Where did he go? He had disappeared, perhaps being a bush to take a leak. Or, so I thought. But no bushes were in sight. But I could smell the foul stench of Inquisitional urine.

I opened the front door, walked to my room, and pondered this preternatural experience.

Then I realized that I had in my hand Torquemada's book. You know, the one he was clutching to his chest on the subway.

I opened the book to the title page. Its title was: The Inquisition's Little Book of Bile.

I began to read it. What a shock this was. It was a manual to guide Butch and MacGuigan for their upcoming Inquisition of Brian Tiffen.

Here are the main points of Torquemada's Little Book of Bile.

1) The accused will never be told, nor can he ever know the accusations against him.

2) The accused can never confront his accusers, nor know who they are.

3) The accused is guilty from the start. No judicial process can remove the guilt.

4) All judicial decisions are final. They cannot be reversed. These can never be appealed. Final is final.

5) The preferred sentence is death by burning at the stake.

1. If the accused is a Jew, he may request baptism into the Catholic religion. Then, this will be followed by strangulation. The corpse of the Jew then will be burned at the stake in an auto de fe, in a fire in the city square.

2. If you are a converso (a Jew or a Moslem) who is faking a conversion to Catholicism, you do not have the choice of baptism followed by strangulation. Instead you will be burned alive while tied to a stake, until dead. Then your corpse will be disemboweled by a certified papal guard.

6) If anyone reads these instructions from the Little Book of Bile, and then reveals them to others, he himself will be apprehended

and disemboweled. His corpse will then be impaled on a tall iron pike at the city gates, for eight weeks during the season of Lent. Then his remains will be dressed in magic underwear, and buried in perpetuity in a deep salt mine, somewhere in the state of Utah.

To understand the context of the Inquisition of the Father Brian Tiffen, S.J., I need to fill you in on who Father Haring was, and what his influence was on Vatican II.

The most significant way that Vatican II hit Regis College was by a book titled The Law of Christ (and a thick one at that) by a German Redemptionist Priest named Father Bernard Haring. Its theme was direct: Love, and love alone is the answer to all the problems of God's People. He didn't badmouth Sheridan's version of moral theology and the empty natural law. Father Haring's message was simple: We are the People of God. Christ is our Savior, and Christ loves us, the People of God. What's to worry?

The endless and moronic distinctions about Onanism and birth control are just a waste of time. Give it up, guys, Love is the answer.

Father Haring was ordained before the start of World War II. Then he was drafted into the German Army as a chaplain and a medic. Against orders, he ministered to soldiers of all faiths. It was then that he developed the notion that love is the answer. After the war he continued his ministry with former soldiers. He came to develop an ecumenical point of view much wider than that of Roman Catholicism.

He began teaching moral theology at the Redemptorist College in Rome.

And then he wrote his book.

And by the time Vatican II came into play, his writing had informed the thinking of many of the big guns visiting the Vatican. These guys are thinking: maybe there is a better way.

Certainly, Roncalli (Pope John XXIII) was moved by Haring's example and writing. Also, the American and Canadian diocesan priests read his book and used its message for their pastoral care. In fact, in 1965, during the summer I spent at Gonzaga University after my ordination to the priesthood, Father Haring gave a two week lecture series based on his book. The place was jam packed. For me this was a once in a lifetime experience. It pulled together all the positive aspects of Vatican II.

I went to confession to him in his room at Gonzaga. Really, it was like going to confession to Jesus Himself. You could feel that Father Haring was a truly holy man. Any problem a penitent might have about telling the truth, or really confessing his sins just seemed to vanish. Kneeling down by the side of Father Haring, truth-telling and sin-conscious issues simply did not arise. It was a moment of grace that I never forgot.

Brothers and Sisters, Father Haring's spirit is all over Vatican II. But you won't hear about him in the official baloney printed about Vatican II. The old guard didn't see it coming, so Cardinal Ottaviani went ahead and poisoned John XXIII anyway. The spirit of Christ slipped back into the clutches of the Vatican money launderers.

Stay with me now. I have a point and I will get to it.

Remember what I told you about casus conscientiae (a case of conscience): a classroom exercise in splitting hairs about some contrived moral problem. Only two people at Regis College believed in this artificial mechanism of casus conscientiae. They were – who else? - Butch Sheridan and Father Elliott MacGuigan.

The schedule is that during a scholastic's fourth year of theology (the kid is already ordained a priest), each must make presentation of a casus, concocted by Butch or MacGuigan. This is the hierarchy's last shot at testing the scholastic's orthodoxy. These were held after supper in a large classroom.

The night in question was the turn of Father Brian Tiffin, S.J. He was a year ahead of me. He was a tall, skinny mathematician and disciple of Bernand Lonergan's, S.J. book Insight, and, wonderful to relate, Father Bernard Haring's book The Law of Christ.

The event was designed to be uneventful. Everyone expects this will be smooth. There will be no bumps on the road. Butch and MacGuigan sit in the front row since it really is their show.

I sat at a desk one row back. Something is going to "go off." I sense that all is not right about Brian Tiffen, and I want to be an eyewitness to the impending carnage in that room, which for once does not involve Butch and Mike Casey.

The thing is, Brian Tiffin is not the meek lamb led to slaughter that Mike Casey, his lips sealed, has thus far been.

Brian stepped up to the podium but did not sit at the desk. He stood tall, skinny, and fearless.

He read off the casus that Butch and MacGuigan had given him. He said a few mumbling words about it, and indeed the casus itself was trivial and insignificant.

Then Brian began to praise Father Lonergan for his rejuvenation of dogmatic theology. "What a great reform of the stale Thomism Father Lonergan has performed for us," he said.

Then came the bombshell. "It's a pity that some Jesuit moral theologian hasn't done the same job of renovation, and reforming of moral theology itself, from top to bottom. And I mean especially in the manner of Bernard Haring, the Redemptorist from Germany. Moral theology is still stuck in its old ways, nothing but legalisms, Old Testament thinking, and sterile distinctions about excommunications, and wasted seed. No one thinks like that anymore. How can I go forth as a priest, and preach that old stuff?"

Then he added, "The Church is renewing itself with liturgy in the vernacular, and with new scriptural studies and understanding of the message of Christ. It's about time that moral theology caught up with the Spirit of Vatican II, the way Father Haring has done with his book The Law of Christ. Pope John XXIII while he was alive made Father Haring's book the basis of the entire work, pastoral especially, of the Council."

Brian had his say.

And then the carnage began. MacGuigan's face was beet red and he seemed to gasp for air.

Then Butch strapped on his bayonet and charged full tilt at Brian.

"You have no right to say what you just said. Father Haring's book is not reliable, it's probably heretical. You can't trust that priest. He is going against all the teaching of the Roman Catholic and Apostolic Church since the Council of Trent four hundred years ago. He can't be trusted. He's like Luther all over again. And do we need that? Never!" And he then smacked the edge of his hand on the desk.

Brian recoiled a bit. Even so he did not budge. "Father Haring's teaching has been a real help to me, and I..."

Butch started in again. "This is dangerous doctrine you're saying. There is no authority for it. I don't want to hear anymore of it." Brian was lucky that Butch did not have his axe-head with him.

Then MacGuigan recovered from his shock. He started to yell, "You're a menace! You're a menace! You will do harm to Catholics with this Love is the answer. The Church cannot function without the guidance of canon law. Those canons were worked out centuries ago, and have made the Roman Church the only bulwark against heresy and the Communist attacks on the papacy. And the sanctity of marriage and virginity."

I sat in a state of terror. My body ached with Brian's.

But Brian would not budge.

MacGuigan again took up the chant. "You're a menace, a menace. You should be ashamed!"

There were about sixty guys in the room. Attendance was mandatory. Guys were hardly breathing and were shriveled with fear and parched throats.

Only one man in that room had any guts. Only Brian Tiffen had a clean slate.

Let me tell you this: That evening Father Haring's message and indeed the Spirit of Christ that was prompting the Vatican Council, took a severe battering.

Every denunciation carries with it a threat. This could happen to anyone of us there. Butch and MacGuigan marched out, like a couple of thugs victorious in a street fight. The rest of us slowly filed out of the room. No one was talking.

The guys returned in silence to their rooms. But I wandered down the hall towards the front entrance. I had to get outside and breathe some fresh air.

But before I got there I heard some talking and chattering near the entrance. I turned and stared in that direction. There was MacGuigan and Sheridan. They were smoking cigars and sipping brandy. And also a third figure was there, gesticulating widely and making guttural sounds. He was saying, "Hip, hip, hooray! Put Tiffen On The Bonfire Today!"

Torquemada, MacGuigan, and the Butcher – celebrating the evening of Nacht und Nebul.

CHAPTER 35: THE DEATH OF MAMA

My second year at Regis College, 1963-64, is mostly a blur. Oscar hangs around me a lot. I play the guitar and sing folk songs. This is some distraction from growing awareness that my Jesuit religious life is hopeless. Oscar's obsession with me continues. I gradually acquire some skill at telling him to back off.

Kennedy gets shot in Dallas. The entire world groans. Johnson goes after Vietnam. I get into loud arguments with Bernie Bush and other heroes (there are many) of Anti-Communist baloney. My feelings of helplessness seem to mirror the world insanity.

The dogmatic theology classes, now called Christology, are abysmal. Moral Theology and Canon Law, Bleh! – Need I say more? The promises of Vatican Two trickle down to us. Pope John XXIII (Roncalli) is bumped off by Cardinal Ottaviani a few months before

Kennedy. The Diem brothers are snuffed. Everything is death, and I'm feeling it.

I looked in the mirror. Here's what it said: "Casey, you look like shit." Father Dave Aslein, the Spiritual Father, says I need to go away for a while.

I am sent to the Canadian Jesuit Novitiate in Guelph, Ontario. There I go for long walks in the snow. I recreate only with the ordained priests there, many of whom are aged and retired. I do all of this without cigarettes.

One old geezer Jesuit has a newspaper clipping reporting that off the coast of Scotland a man was swallowed by a whale, and then after several days was barfed back onto the beach. The old geezer exclaims that, "See, the Book of Jonah is proven true." He says this in the middle of the twentieth century.

Jesus, I need cigarettes. I even think of trying to pray, even the rosary; maybe, I am nuts. There are no pills for my condition, and so I return to Regis College.

Then it's insomnia, but no sobbing of the guts.

Next up is the confessional exam; you know, when the priest sits in the wooden closet and forgives sins.

Me? Really, I get to forgive sins? Me? Come on, me with my dick in my hand? It can't be. But I pass the exam.

At the end of the year, Oscar is ordained a priest. He then flies to Spokane for the summer for college courses in counseling. He also visits my parents often. My mother just loves him, Papa can't stand him.

I repair for the summer to the Canadian Jesuit villa on Lake Muskoka, near Gordon Bay. Every day I row a boat to a secluded cove a couple of miles away. The hillside is a massive slab of granite. About one hundred feet up the slope I find my spot. The granite is bare and warm. My clothes are off and the god Apollo beams down on me the entire day. I am as dark as a Greek. The forces of nature nurse me back to some equilibrium.

Then it's back to the villa for supper and watching the Vietnam War on T.V. Next I begin my nightly reading of The Classics of Analytic Philosophy. This reading is not escapism. I am very serious about penetrating what it really is about. I make notes and outlines.

About this time I begin to get letters from Mama. These are about Dominic. His health is very bad. Diabetes from the age of three, and insulin shots three times a day. Mama's letters are despondent. She says God does not hear her prayers. You can read about the effects of Dominic and diabetes on Mama and the Casey Family in my book, Where I Come From, (on Amazon).

When I get back to Regis College for the 1964-65 school year (at the end of which I will be ordained a priest) her letters continue.

I keep trying to make a deal with God about a miracle for Dominic's health. Dave Aslein counsels me that there can be no deals with God. Instead I must pray and pray and pray. Thanks a lot, God.

I'm trying as hard as I can to get interested in the Scriptures. Father Dave Stanley teaches the course on Letters of St. Paul. It's not about what these letters mean, but about what they are. It's called Form Criticism. This is a dose of rationality in the swampy waters of traditional piety. And so I'm thinking, maybe I can make sense of it all.

Oscar is back from Spokane and fills me in on what a wonderful time he had with Mama and Papa in Spokane.

I'm feeling awful, very guilty. But I have no idea of what I'm guilty of. In some class, I sit in the back row because I'm feeling uncontrollable sadness. I just start to blubber, and by the time I get outside the building, I'm in a steady and heavy blubbering.

What is this? Am I going nuts? This is not the volcanic sobbing of the guts. It's a steady tidal movement of tears and snot. I walk around the grounds for a couple of hours, always blubbering and sobbing. I stay out on the grounds by myself all through lunch and after.

This continues for several days, and no one knows of it. Naturally, I think of these tears as a sign of weakness. It does not occur to me that they are a message or a signal that the end is near.

Indeed the end is near. It really is. It's not my end, but my mother's.

I can just tell.

Then, one night after supper, Father Minister knocks on my door. I have an urgent phone call from my father.

On the phone, Papa tells me that Mama is in Sacred Heart Hospital, and that she'll be gone soon. I start to cry and so does Papa. His wife, my mother, who has been the source of my entire spiritual life, is near the end.

I say, "I'm coming home." Papa and Michael flood the phone lines with tears and protestations that this cannot be. It just can't happen.

The next day I'm on the plane to Spokane. When I get there, Dominic meets me at the airport. We go to the hospital. Papa, Margaret and Patty are there. This is for real.

My sister Margaret, who is much more aware of essential issues than I am, later told me that when I came into Mama's hospital room, Mama's face lit up and she smiled at the sight of me. Margaret says that after that Mama felt o.k. about dying.

Mama's sister Ione and her brothers Hank and Leo are in and out for the next day or so. Grandma Daisey Grant, Mama's mother, also appears but seems quite uncomfortable at Sacred Heart Hospital.

For a couple of days Papa and I and Dominic wander around in a daze. We don't really talk about stuff. We all keep going back to the corridor at Sacred Heart Hospital and just stand there silent. Margaret and Patty and Mama's sister Ione keep watch inside.

I notice that Uncle Hank is in the corridor is weeping. Then a chaplain arrives in a white frock and goes into Mama's room. In a little bit he comes out and walks away. Some hospital staff arrive and close the door. Other staff herd us all away to some room, and we sit.

It's over, and there will be no getting over it.

Mama died on October 24th, 1964, three months shy of her sixtieth birthday.

Margaret subsequently told me that she was holding Mama's head up for a drink of water when she died. It was peaceful, blessed, and she just slipped away. Margaret also told me that if I had arrived from Toronto a week later, Mama would have lived a week longer, so much did Micheal the Jesuit mean to her.

Two days later it's time for the Rosary at Hennessey's Funeral Parlor. Since Papa is paying for the entire funeral service, I am designated to lead the Rosary.

It is by far the worst rosary devotion I've ever led. But the huge crowd at Hennessey's wants and expects the ritual. I endure it.

Hennessey's is packed with the People of God, the real people of God. No Jesuits, except me, are present. But all the people whose elderly parents Mama attended at St. Joseph's Old Folks Home were there to pay Mama their respects. All the nuns from Margaret's religious order have driven over from Seattle, plus all the Jesuit Mothers' Club (a money-raising organization) are present (she had been the President several times). But Father Prange, S.J., the pastor at St.

Aloysius is not. The parking lot is filled and folk must park up and down Division Street.

Who knew? Come on, who knew? Mama was a centrifugal force, and I for one merely suspected this. But now I knew. Papa, who went to many funerals at Hennessey's later, said it was one of the largest crowds there in recent years.

At Catholic funerals, at least then, during and after the Rosary, the box is kept open. And all present file past. It took almost an hour for the People of God to pass by the box of this woman and mother who had forced us out of the North Dakota tundra and gopher holes to Spokane so we could get a Catholic education. She did this against all economic odds and Dominic's diabetes.

At first she was a hot lunch cook at parish schools. Then she was a licensed practical nurse. It was bedpans and making beds at Sacred Heart Hospital. Then she took over as the chief nurse at St. Joseph's Old Folks Home, more bed pans and actually running the entire operation there for the Providence Order of Sisters.

Until her body just gave out.

She died of breast cancer and liver cancer. Her cancer and death was a harsh verdict on a life of devoted service.

But I say she died of excessive Catholicism. Margaret and I both agree about this.

The Rosary service is over. Now it's time for the Casey family to get into Hennessey's hearse to drive back to Papa's house on Astor Street. I and Dominic are the last two to get in the wagon. I'm about to crawl in and Dominic is behind me, when Michael Casey erupts in a deep and terrifying groan. A high volume groan wrenches my entire physical frame. I had never heard any sound so ultimate and shuddering. It is a preternatural sound that is deeper than the sobbing of the guts. The rest of the family becomes alarmed.

It goes on. Dominic is behind me and tries to help me. My knees are slipping down onto the wagon's running board. I groan and sob beyond any control.

The end of Mama, the end of Michael. Void and bottomless aching. The temple veil is rent in two as the Old World rests in Mama's box. Myself, I stagger into the nether world of darkness and shadow.

The next day the funeral is to be held at St. Aloysius Church. Father Prange, S.J., and another Jesuit priest officiate. For this they will each get a stipend. Nice, huh?

The night before, Grandma Daisey Grant stayed at Papa's house. The funeral is at nine a.m. Hennessey's wagon will pick all of us up and we'll travel in a body to the church.

Grandma Daisey has an immovable grievance and disgust at the Church. When the Grants moved to Spokane in 1927, and Mama remained in North Dakota married to Papa, the Irishman Matt Casey. Grandma Daisey and Grandpa Henry Grant lived a few blocks from Sacred Heart Hospital. The Hospital employed both as dishwashers. This was around the beginning of the Great Depression, and they felt lucky to get the job.

But Grandma Daisey would eat the food off the returned dinners and suppers. This is real poverty behavior. It's below even riding the Greyhound. One day, the nun in charge of the kitchen caught Daisey in the act of scooping the uneaten Jell-O into her mouth.

The nun blasted Daisey on the spot, and the next day both Daisey and Grandpa Henry were terminated. I had heard this story as a youngster in Parshall. Two proud people out of work because of some unsanctified Jell-O. They never again went inside a Catholic Church. Mama was the only Grant (of two brothers and four sisters) who stuck with the Church. Because of Mama's deep commitment to the Catholic Church, the Grants always seemed, to me at least, alienated from Mama.

An hour or so before we all get in the funeral wagon, I sat down with Grandma Daisey, and asked her if she would like to sit in the front row close to the coffin, and maybe even take communion with the rest of us.

Daisey said, "No, I'll just sit in the back row, and then ride with you all to the graveyard."

Clueless, I asked again, and she said, "Michael, this is the second child I've lost." Mama's much younger sister, Inez, had died in 1934 at the age of fourteen. She had a sudden onset of Bright's disease (liver) and died at home within twenty-four hours.

Daisey was softly weeping. I shut up. The wagon arrived. We all got in and went to the Church. Next, it's to Holy Cross Cemetery for the burial. The box was lowered into the ground. It was several rows away from the grave site of Inez, her sister.

Figure 12 Margaret, Grandma Daisey, and Michael

Figure 13 The Day Mama died. Margaret Papa, Patty, Michael and Dominic

Figure 14 Mama, 1927, in North Dakota

Figure 15 Mama and her country school class, in Mountrail, North Dakota

CHAPTER 36: ORDINATION TO THE PRIESTHOOD

I hang out in Spokane with Papa for several weeks. He seemed to be in good shape. I was a hollowed out scarecrow after the funeral. What was left for me?

I returned to Toronto to finish my third year of theology, and eventually ordination to the priesthood. Stuff went on at Regis, but it was not theology. It was about Civil Rights and the Vietnam War. You can't believe the reactionaries lurking in the shadows, pictures of Cardinal Spellman, the American Pope, getting off a plane from Vietnam with Madam Nu, Diem's sister-in-law. (Spellman and the Madam, are they together?). The Catholic MacNamara, the nihilist MacGeorge Bundy, and big ears Johnson hulking over all. What could anyone believe in?

There was the Vatican Two Council. From its endless blather came the news that the Mass would be in the vernacular. We all are uplifted. Maybe there can be some progress. Also, there was quiet talk among the unordained that the deadening birth control doctrine will be modified. Paul VI said a committee would decide.

I can hardly wait for the school year to end, exams taken, and a plane boarded for a trip flight back to Spokane for ordination. All the Oregonians will be ordained there in St. Aloysius Church, next to Gonzaga University. It's just a few blocks away from the Casey home from which I left for the Jesuits in 1952.

Figure 16 Ordination Photo, 1964

The actual ordination ceremony goes ever so smooth, a mere three hours wrapped in a white linen chasuble. I think I know what's going on. Papa, Margaret, and Dominic of course are there. My Casey cousins from North Dakota show up, Dick and Bob with their wives and children, and also Mary Catherine, their sister, with her kids and husband Pee Wee Carlson from Montana.

My older sister Patty, her kids, and husband Eugene Buckmaster, who had received time off from his duties in the U.S. Air Force to attend are there. Also, my nephews, Richard, Michael, John, David, and my niece Margaret all are there. Oscar Mendez is present and schmoozing with all the Casey Klan. And many nuns from Margaret's religious order, St. Joseph's of Newark. In family terms, it's a very big deal.

I was always proud, very proud of being a Casey. But this Casey gathering really lifted me up. It made me feel that after all I was O.K., even though I was a Jesuit.

None of Mama's side of the family is there. Well, no wonder, since they left the Church thirty-five years ago, and will not be coming back after the cheap Jell-O episode at Sacred Heart Hospital with

Grandma Daisey taking the hit from the nun. How about that peonage doctrine?

In the Jesuit mythology ordination to the priesthood was supposed to be the greatest thing that could ever happen to a guy; you know, like the discovery of gold in the Klondike, the Big El Dorado, the Treasure of Sierra Madre, the guarantee that your life would be forever meaningful. You'll be set apart and raised above the rest of God's People.

Well, there was at least one Mickey, the sacred oil still wet on his fingers, for whom the entire business went bone dry after a couple of months. The euphoria dried up, and the aforesaid Mickey remembered who he was: just a guy who ached and ached for his Mama.

I spent the summer of 1965 at Gonzaga University. Papa worked there as a janitor and I visited with him everyday. On weekends I traveled to parishes in eastern Washington and northern Idaho taking the resident pastor's place when he went on vacation. I'm hearing confessions before Mass and preaching a sermon during it.

Towards the end of August I returned to Toronto. It's back to Muskoka Lake and on weekends I again fill in as visiting pastor at the small churches in the various parishes nearby.

Muskoka is all tourist country, many folk traveling there from New York or upstate New York. These folk want to go to confession away from their home parish. These confessions last for hours. In one place on the Lake, there is a chapel with some pews and the rest is folding chairs. But there is no confessional box. A chair is set for the priest near the communion rail, but no curtain, just a kneeler for the penitent. I hold my left hand like a blinker by my left eyeball so that I cannot see who is confessing. The folk there seem to accept this. But I am very uncomfortable with it. It just does not look good.

It is in this setting that I hear the plaintive sounds of the voices of the faithful. Very few of these voices are male voices; guys don't go to confession very often. As a result, I hear the seductive voices of the younger females.

But I do not move my blinkering hand. Please realize that I am not a man of steel. I never look but, Jesus, this exercise in self-control is exhausting.

And, now to think that in a few years, the Pope, Paul VI, will abolish individual confession, and proclaim that only group confession is necessary for Absolution.

I want to write a letter to Paul VI and ask him, "Hey, Pope, how many confessions like this did you hear? Did you hear the voices of the young women, and if so, what were you experiencing? Yeah, sure, your Holiness, no hard-ons at all. Yeah, sure. Listen to me, Paul VI, just why was individual confession abolished, in favor of silent group confession?"

"Exactly, you were not a man of steel, and couldn't handle the sultry voices."

At least some good came out of Paul VI's homosexual papacy: individual confession of sins was dumped.

CHAPTER 37: HOW MIKE CASEY FINALLY LEFT THE JESUITS

In September of 1965 my last school year at Regis College began. I am an ordained priest, and therefore of some monetary value to the Jesuits in Toronto. Accordingly, every weekend Father Minister sends me out to various Toronto parishes to hear confessions on Saturday afternoon and night, and to preach three or four sermons on Sunday, and say Mass three times on Sunday morning.

By now Father Minister (remember him of Look Magazine infractions?) thinks I'm a great guy. These diocese pastors want me back for another tour of duty, and Father Minister loves those two hundred dollars a weekend stipends that I bring back and sign over to him. The Mickey is a cash cow, despite gallons of wasted spermatozoa.

And, hey, another thing: Father Ed Sheridan is no longer Rector of Regis College. His term of six years was up in August. His replacement was Father John Hochbein, S.J. It's looking good, isn't it?

Father Hochbein is not a moral theologian. He is not a canon lawyer. He is not a very good teacher (no depth). But he is a very warm man, likes to smoke, and just loves the premium Canadian whiskey my two hundred dollars a weekend check pays for. Actually he is a warm-hearted Bavarian. If you compare the sadist Sheridan to the Bavarian beer meister, what is there to choose?

When it's time for the dreaded manifestation of conscience to him by the now ordained Father Mike Casey, S.J. I'm thinking it will be a breeze.

So, call me the Breeze.

But the Breeze becomes the blubbering and sobbing of the guts when it's my turn to enter his office for the yearly manifestation of conscience.

I entered his office on the first anniversary of Mama's death on October 24th, 1965. I sit and notice that the hated axe-head is missing. (Did Butch need it elsewhere? Are there heads in his care still unsevered?)

In Hochbein's room, it's a replay of my time with Father George a couple of years ago. The sobbing of the guts all over again.

Father Hochbein intones, "How's it going, Mike?" He has just snuffed out his cigarette.

The dam bursts, and gallons of my pent-up emotional fluid pour out. Hochbein is startled by the victim slumped in front of him. "Sob, ahg..., sob, ahg..., sob, ahg..."

The waters are gushing from my eyes. These are enough to flood the suburb of Willowdale. My unconscious eruption of agony, guilt, and misplaced anger unnerve Hochbein. I'm not as loud as I was at Mama's Rosary, but, Jesus, large puddles of water form on Hochbein's floor.

He tries feeding me Kleenex, and soon there is a large pile of them sopping wet on the floor.

After some time I get some articulation out. "I feel so guilty. My mother, Papa, my family, Dominic's diabetes....agh, sob...I don't wanna live like this."

Brothers and Sisters, you can trust the unconscious to speak the truth, once it's time to come out of the closet. But that actual time is not predictable.

I spent maybe an hour in Hochbein's office. I am a wet kitchen rag used over and over, and wrung out again and again

Brothers and Sisters in Christ, it's time for me to plain get out of the prison, the nuthouse, away from the Jesuit KGB, the lunatic and sadist Sheridan, the mindless natural law. Fuck it all, I'm getting out.

Folks, that was the ballgame right there. The score is: Jesuits thirteen (years) and Mike Casey zero.

In a few days, discussions on high were held, decisions came down: Mike Casey has to go away. He must recuperate in a warmer climate.

In a few more days, Father Minister gets ahold of me, and says, "Get your stuff together. Tomorrow at nine a.m., I'm driving you to the Toronto Airport. You're going to the Jesuit Mission in Jamaica. That's in the Caribbean, you know. You'll like it."

I'm physically weak still from the sobbing and emotional breakdown in Hochbein's office. (I guess I really scared the shit out of Hochbein.) But I stick some items in my bag and the next morning I'm on a plane to Jamaica. I arrive there, and the Jesuits put me up at their high school in Kingston.

There is no more sobbing or tears. But, really, things have happened very fast, and I often wonder in my enforced idleness, if I am losing my mind. It's all fog and unknowing. I really do think I'm losing my mind. If I have another breakdown, hell, I'll just have to commit myself to the looney bin.

After a few weeks at the high school in Kingston, some Jesuit drives me and others to the north shore of Jamaica. The Jesuits own a very nice villa there (a house, actually) in a secluded compound at St. Ann's Bay. The villa is a retreat where the Jesuits in Jamaica can stay as they recuperate from their missionary labors.

There is an interim Jesuit Superior at the villa. He assigns me to various weekend "missions" into the mountains, where I am the only white person seen for months. On Sundays I put on priest stuff, say mass, hear confessions, etc. The native Jamaicans get a big kick out of me. They are very warm and demonstrative. I like them and they like me.

I also travel the length of the island performing similar duties. Once I rode a bus, named the "Honey Bee," from Port Antonio (on the east end of the island) back to St. Ann's Bay. As usual, I'm the only white guy on it, but there was no friction.

Then, sometime around the middle of February, while I'm "recuperating" at the villa, there comes a phone call to me from the Oregon Province Headquarters. I'm told I must return immediately to Seattle because my sister Margaret is near death.

I am told no details but the Jesuit caller assures me that this is so. My father had contacted him.

The next day I'm on the plane from Montego Bay flying to New Orleans. Next it's a very long flight to San Francisco, a lay-over, and then onto Seattle. Dominic met me at the airport, and drove me to Providence Hospital.

Margaret was in a coma. She had been in a coma for several days. It's looking grim.

Papa, Dominic, and Michael stand around, waiting. A doctor explains that Margaret has an unknown medical condition, and he's looking for some medicine for it. Meanwhile, because of the condition, Margaret had lost all the hair on her head. It had been burned out by a nasty fever.

This is not the time for the sobbing of the guts. But I do have a fierce pain in my gut. Dominic and I talk, but not about deep stuff.

Papa's eyes are like balloons filled with water. But he manages to flirt with some nurses and nuns from Margaret's Religious Order.

It's been a year and a half since Mama died. I daren't think the question: who's next?

A day or so later the virus lifted. Margaret rallied out of the coma, and started talking and drinking water and juices. In a few more days, she was O.K., minus her hair.

The doctor wrote a medical paper on Margaret's condition. I think the medical condition was named after Margaret.

In time, Margaret returned to her convent, and resumed teaching the eighth grade on Mercer Island near Seattle.

The pain in my gut did not diminish, and I had to eat only Cream of Wheat with skim milk. But I didn't quit smoking cigarettes.

Papa and I drove over to Spokane. I stayed at his house on Astor Street.

Dominic returned to Tacoma, where he lived and worked as a diesel mechanic.

I did not return to Regis College.

I was told to forget about it. Someone from Jesuit headquarters assigned me to an Indian Mission in Washington State. And, I never missed Regis College.

In August of 1966 Dominic died of complications of infantile diabetes. He was twenty-six years old.

In 1967 to 1969, I taught philosophy at Seattle University. There, I hung out with Father Toulouse. The word there was that he was still the same as he was in Spokane in 1950-51. I even met some of the young boys involved. I did not witness any of his misdeeds. But I suspected it. The effect of this on me was that I resolved to get away from the Jesuits and Seattle University altogether. Enough, I say, of Jesuit infamy.

Rev. Michael Casey, S.J.

Figure 17 Michael, at Seattle University 1967

There you have it, folks, it was actually my family, Mama's death, and Margaret's near-death, that got me out of the Jesuit Order. In March of 1969, I walked out of the door of Seattle University, and the Jesuit Order. I never have considered going back, and I signed no laicisation papers to that effect. I just walked away. Several times, various Jesuits have tracked me down, and said there are some papers I should sign. You can imagine what I told them. Autonomy once discovered is just precious.

Papa remarried in 1970. He was divorced six months later. In 1969, I married Suzanne Schack. We were married for eight years. I have two children, Kristina and Dawn.

Margaret left the convent in 1984, and goes to every protest rally she can find, especially if the Pope is against it.

And now I have five grandchildren, each a spectacular beauty of intellect and prowess. Their names are: Zoe Mae, Finn Michael, Walker, Kelsey, and Piper Lily. On my car, I have a bumper sticker that says: MY KIDS HAVE BETTER VALUES THAN YOUR KIDS. AND THEY MAKE MORE MONEY.

My daughter Dawn looks and acts exactly like my mother.

And although it took my mother's death for me to swing it, I no longer think that black is white.

Figure 18 Michael with his two daughters, Kristina (left) and Dawn (right)

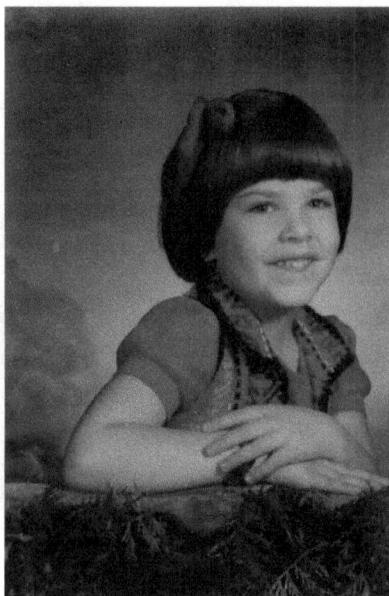

Figure 19 Dawn in Kindergarten

Figure 20 Kristina in high school

Figure 21 Michael's grandchildren: Walker, Finn, Zoe, Kelsey, and Piper

Figure 22 Michael's daughters: Dawn (left) and Kristina (right)

Figure 23 1969, Papa, Margaret, Michael and his wife, Suzanne Schack

EPILOGUE

Karmic Ironies

The Jesuits sold St. Francis Xavier Novitiate at Sheridan in the early 1970s. The purchaser was none other than the Church of Scientology.

From Jesuit mind control to the E-meter, huh? Some things never change.

About the same time, the Federal Government built a federal penitentiary on the outskirts of the town of Sheridan. The chaplain of the prison at the bottom of the hill was Father John McBride, S.J. John was a classmate of mine in the Jesuits back in 1952. I mention him in chapter seven.

John had been through the Battle of the Bulge in 1944. He was an eighteen year-old private in the front line. The loss of life was in the thousands. In time he was also a first lieutenant in the Korean War, again in the front line. He was wounded and returned to the States. I remember that he was a ROTC instructor at Gonzaga University.

John felt called to the priesthood and to the Jesuits. At Sheridan, he walked with a bit of a limp, the effects of a wound from the Korean War.

I also remember that he was a most positive influence on me personally. Since he was from Coeur d'Alene, Idaho (just across the state line from Spokane), he and I had a lot in common to talk about. My recollections of him are only good. Also, we are both very Irish.

The portrayal of the Jesuits that I have given in these pages do not apply to him; in fact, just the opposite.

From 1952 at the top of the hill to the bottom of the hill is the first part of this irony.

The second part of this irony concerns a prisoner at the prison in Sheridan. His name is Father Bill Bichsel, S.J. He was always known as "Bix".

He is also a case of "from the top of the hill to the bottom of the hill." Bix had joined the Jesuits in 1948, and had "served" four years at the Novitiate. I was very good friends with Bix during the time I was teaching at Seattle University. We hung out together and ran with the same crowd. I left the Jesuits and Bix stayed.

Soon Bix found a courageous outlet for his Jesuit vocation. He became a protester against the CIA and the Reagan war in Central America. He also inspired some nuns and lay persons to protest with him.

As I recall, the protest that landed him in jail took place in front of the CIA's School of the Americas. He and others splashed blood on a sign in front of the school. This is the school that trained mercenaries for the war in Central America. Once, these mercenaries had invaded the Jesuit school in San Salvador, and murdered five Jesuit priests, their housekeeper and her daughter. The same murderers had also shot and killed the Bishop of San Salvador, Bishop Romero, while he was saying Mass.

Bill could not stand by in silence, as all the other Jesuits in the USA did. He launched his real calling as a protester against War.

Indeed, a federal judge sentenced him to prison. That's how he came to be at the bottom of the hill at Sheridan. Bix has been in prison many times since then. He just won't quit. Once he was in solitary confinement for a month, and went on a hunger fast there.

Bix's example hung over the Casey family in one way or another. He had been one of my brother's teachers in high school. Bix was also good friends with my father, Matt Casey. I know papa talked about him a lot.

My sister, Margaret Mary Casey, having left the convent, became a vigorous peace protester and peace activist, and participated with Bix and others in front of the nuclear base on the Olympic Peninsula at Bangor, Washington.

But Margaret was never sentenced to jail since she had already served twenty-seven years in a convent, under the constant surveillance of Mother Superior.

As I have said, never underestimate the power of example. A worthy example becomes, in some quiet way, part of your own spirit and character. John McBride has followed a path of courage and wise counsel to the rejects of society. And Bix was a forceful example for the many folk who thirst for justice and peace. Margaret herself is on every protest and picket line in the Northwest, and also even in Washington, D.C., and New York City; always for women's rights, and lately in front of the Archbishop's residence in Seattle, calling for fairness and restitution for the victims of the ugly priestly pedophile scandal in the Catholic Church.

Bix, John, and Margaret are dedicated and genuine.

Myself, I had a calling as a teacher, owing no doubt to my mother's example in front of me. I stayed with teaching. I taught undergraduate philosophy at a community college. You might call it remedial metaphysics. My heart was in the job, and I left all I had in the classroom. I don't know what my influence was, but it was a calling of the spirit.

I don't consider my life to be a life of faith. But it has been a life of spirit. And for this I am grateful.

After the Jesuits, the Caseys

Figure 24 Michael's family with Patty's family, Papa (left) and Margaret (right)

Figure 25 Eugene and Patty Buckmaster and Michael's family

Figure 26 Kristina

Figure 27 Dawn

Figure 28 Finn

Figure 29 Walker

Figure 30 Piper

Figure 31 Kelsey (left), Piper (center), and Zoe (right)

Figure 32 Finn (left) and Walker (right)

Figure 33 Kelsey

385

Figure 34 Zoe

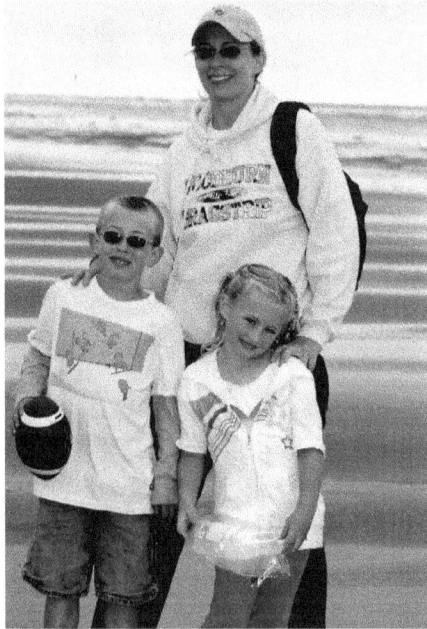

Figure 35 Kristina, Walker (left), and Kelsey (right)

Figure 36 Zoe

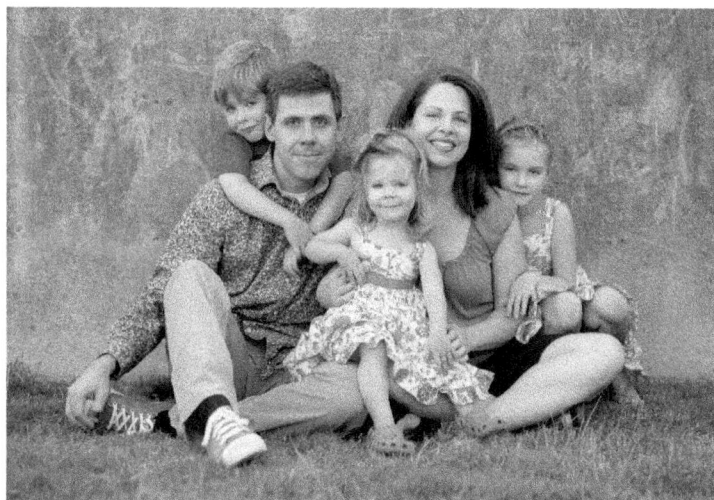

Figure 37 From left: Finn, Morgan, Piper, Dawn, Zoe

My Family Now

Figure 38 Michael Casey 2013

Figure 39 Cinnamon, The Belgian Shepard

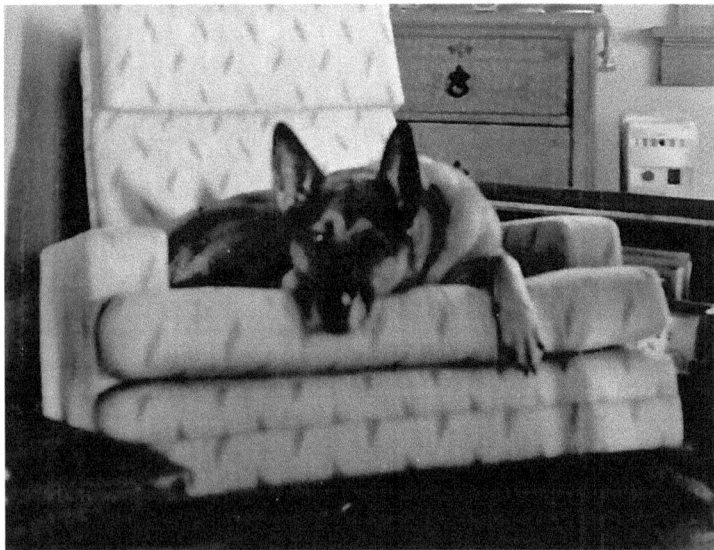

www.ingramcontent.com/pod-product-compliance
Lightning Source LLC
Chambersburg PA
CBHW051411090426
42737CB00014B/2620